Floyd's

100 Great Curries

100 Great Curries
Keith Floyd

Photographs by Neil Barclay

CASSELL ILLUSTRATED

This book is dedicated to the memory of my mother, the best cook ever:

"Win" Phyllis Lorraine Floyd
November 22, 1918–July 24, 2002

With special thanks to Tess Floyd and Barbara Dixon (who has so
patiently edited so many of my books).

First published in Great Britain in 2004 by Cassell Illustrated,
a division of Octopus Publishing Group Limited,
2–4 Heron Quays, London E14 4JP

Text copyright © 2004 Keith Floyd
Design and layout copyright © 2004 Cassell Illustrated

The moral right of Keith Floyd to be identified as the author of this
Work has been asserted in accordance with the Copyright, Designs
and Patents Act of 1988.

Distributed in the United States of America by
Sterling Publishing Co. Inc., 387 Park Avenue South,
New York, NY 10016-8810

A CIP catalog record for this book is available from the
British Library.

ISBN 1 84403 275 2

Keith Floyd is represented by Stan Green Management, Dartmouth,
Devon, UK; telephone +44 1803 770046; fax + 44 1803 770075;
email sgm@clara.co.uk; visit www.keithfloyd.co.uk

Cassell Illustrated would like to thank David Mellor and Paperchase
for the loan of some of the props used in this book.

Printed in China

Contents

Introduction

My mother was a great gardener and a great cook. Every morning, she would tend to the garden, the front with its flowers, and the back where there were neat rows of string beans, fava beans, potatoes, cabbages, carrots, parsnips, purple sprouting broccoli, and, in due season, scallions, radishes, and lettuces. Most of the vegetables she grew from seed. The little patch at the bottom contained tubs of mint and horseradish. There was sage and parsley, thyme and rosemary; there were apples and plums.

After I'd left home, a feast would be waiting whenever I visited my mother. She would say, "I wasn't sure if you would prefer duck or roast leg of lamb with onion sauce, so I have prepared both!" My mother was not one to use gravy granules. The gravy for the duck was made from its giblets, feet, etc., and the gravy for the lamb was made from the roasting juices and vegetable water. Each had its distinctive, natural flavor.

Oh yes, God bless my dear old mom. Her passion and love for food was unrivaled, and without doubt it was my mother's cooking that irrevocably influenced my life and ultimate career. We all miss her terribly—she died in 2002, aged 84.

In her pantry, there were no jars of store-bought brandied jellies, preserves, or pickles, just a row of little cheesecloth-topped jars, with stuck-on handwritten labels, for piccalilli and apple jelly, and screw-topped jars of home-pickled onions, or homemade blackberry and apple or raspberry jelly, for spreading on thick slices of bread and butter at teatime. And, of course, much, much more.

But although, with a few exceptions such as cocoa and tinned salmon, there were no store-bought items in the pantry, there was one can that contained an ocher-brown coarse powder and bore the legend "Madras Curry Powder."

Throughout the week, and week by week, dinner was a rotation of homemade faggots and peas, boiled ham with wax beans and parsley sauce, belly of pork with purple sprouting broccoli or curly kale, and boiled breast of lamb with caper sauce; on Friday nights, we always had braised pigs' trotters served with coarse salt, pepper, and vinegar and thick slices of bread (no butter because the trotters were so fatty and gelatinous it was not required); sometimes on a Monday a shepherd's pie made from the leftover Sunday joint, and then, sometimes, and particularly after Christmas, when the turkey had been served hot on Christmas Day and cold on Boxing Day, the ubiquitous Madras curry powder would come out and pieces of cooked turkey, lamb, or beef were stirred into this gritty, ocher-colored sauce. Curry, it was called! Served with boiled rice with side dishes of dry unsweetened coconut, banana slices, golden raisins, and apple chunks. It was truly revolting. This awful meal would occur at least once a month, but it intrigued me. What was a curry? And then after I started working and joined a local rugby club, I soon discovered the world of Indian restaurants and the Saturday night culture of pints of lager with a Vindaloo. Nowadays, of course, the curry is a thousand times removed from what pleased us all those years ago.

The good thing about curries is that they are really simple and quick to prepare and fun to eat. For the most part, they can be

prepared and frozen for future use and they make great party food—a table groaning with seven or eight different dishes, a range of pickles and chutneys, yogurts and fresh herbs, wonderful breads, lashings of cold lager or ginger beer, or fresh lime juice with sparkling water, pitchers of salted or sweetened lassi, or maybe just cups of green tea. What a party!

And you don't have to be fussy about measuring or weighing ingredients. Cook with your eyes, taste as you cook, dip your finger in. More chiles to make it hotter? Add more chiles. Too hot? Stir in more cream or yogurt. The hottest chiles, used in many of the recipes in this book, are known as Thai chiles— they are very small and very, very hot. The bigger the chile, the milder it is. If you leave the seeds and pith in the chile, it is hotter; with these removed, the dish will be milder. In this book, if the recipe calls for chicken, you don't have to follow that slavishly—you can use lamb, or pork, or beef, or quail! Curries are a moveable feast.

So, here you will find contained over 30 years' worth of hurtling round the globe, learning and enjoying these, some of my favorite curry recipes.

Happy cooking, and may all the wonderful aromas, spices, and flavors of the Orient be with you.

Keith Floyd
Isle sur la Sorgue, France

Curry Culture

At 16, I left school, managed, to get a job and joined a local rugby club. On Saturdays, we would play our game in some lowly division and immediately after the match rush down to the memorial ground in Bristol to watch Bristol Rugby Club thrash any of the top teams in the country. There was always someone who would get us into the clubhouse bar after the game where we could be close to our heroes.

We drank pints and pints of cheap lager until someone said, "It's time for a curry." Up until then, I had never been to an Indian restaurant and I was possibly the youngest member of our side, so ten or twelve of us would invade the Taj Mahal or the Koh-I-Noor—plain, simple places with stained flock wallpaper, Formica tables covered with an invariably equally stained white tablecloth, with cheap glass salt and pepper shakers, and a chrome bowl filled with white sugar lumps. This was in the late 1950s to the early 1960s.

The owner wore a rusty dinner jacket, the shy waiters wore white jackets. There was Chicken or Beef Madras, Vindaloo, and little else: a few European dishes such as T-bone steaks and omelet; there was mango chutney and pappadams—oh, and Bombay Duck, deep-fried smelly dried fish. We would order the hottest dish—in those days, there was no raita, no buttered Indian breads; certainly, Chicken Tikka Masala had not been invented, which, by the way, to this day does not exist in India. There were none of the subtle dishes that we know today. Certainly there was no such thing as a Thai or Malaysian restaurant. The only other curry you might get would be in a Chinese restaurant: a piece of chicken with a hot sauce, not dissimilar to the one my mother made, and often served with fries.

I suppose it was fun and I suppose we enjoyed it, but it wasn't real. Time has moved on. The tandoor oven came to Britain and subtler flavors and tastes emerged. The derogative term "curry house" slipped into obscurity and fine designer Asian restaurants began to appear. Supermarkets introduced ranges of Asian food to cook or reheat at home and curry became big business.

You will find that "curries" are, as far as I know, a British-invented term for spicy dishes; certainly there are no "curries" in India, but there are curries in Malaysia, Thailand, Burma, Africa—in fact. all over the world, all created through interpretation, taste, geographical location, and the availability of spices and produce.

The spicy dishes in this book come from my travels in those countries, and in India, Vietnam, Kashmir, Egypt (yes, they have curries) ,and many other places. Some are wet, some are dry; "curry" is sometimes loosely defined—as in Vietnamese Meat Loaf, a highly spiced meat mixture with fish sauce and chiles—and sometimes immediately recognizable, as in Thai Green Chicken Curry or Lamb Rogan Josh.

The curry has certainly moved on from the lager and Vindaloo days, and we are now able to enjoy many styles of these spicy dishes, as will be seen from the variety and diversity of the recipes in this book.

woks. Stir-frying implements and slotted spoons are handy, as are blenders or food processors.

Before you start cooking your curry, equip yourself with a load of rectangular, plastic boxes or small, glass bowls. Read your recipe carefully. Chop and prepare all your ingredients and place them individually in your bowls in the order in which you add them to the dish. Don't start frying the chicken and then begin to peel the onions. Careful preparation, which can be done hours ahead of cooking time, will ensure that you, as well as your guests, have a good, stress-free time.

The observant among you will notice that I have always put the main ingredient of the recipe first in the ingredients list, and not necessarily in the order in which it is used—this is to remind you when you make your shopping list! A chicken curry isn't much good without the chicken.

A final word of advice. Except when I make my mother's Christmas cake and her Christmas puddings, I never use scales. All the measurements, weights, and cooking times in this book are approximate. Don't follow them slavishly, use common sense, and if you are not already an experienced cook, just rely on a bit of trial and error.

The recipes will generally serve 4–6 people, depending on how hungry you are.

Chicken Curries

This makes a change from good old plain roast chicken.

Vietnamese Roast Chicken with Lemongrass and Tangy Sauce

1 roasting chicken about 3 lb 5 oz–4 lb/ 1.5–1.75 kg

3 stems of lemongrass

6 garlic cloves, peeled

4 shallots, peeled

2 fresh red chiles, deseeded

1 tablespoon sugar

1 tablespoon fish sauce

½ teaspoon salt

a good handful of cilantro leaves, chopped, to garnish

For the tangy sauce

2 garlic cloves, peeled

1 fresh red chile, deseeded

2 tablespoons sugar

2 tablespoons fresh lime juice

2 tablespoons red wine vinegar

2 tablespoons fish sauce

Serves 4–6

First make the tangy sauce by whizzing all the ingredients together in a food processor, then set aside.

Preheat the oven to 425°F/220°C. Put the lemongrass, garlic, shallots, chiles, sugar, fish sauce, and salt into a food processor and whiz until you have a paste.

Using your hands, loosen the chicken skin on the breast and legs and rub half of the lemongrass paste onto the chicken, under the skin. Rub the remaining paste over the chicken skin and into the chicken cavity.

Put the chicken on a roasting rack and roast in the oven for 15 minutes, then reduce the heat to 375°F/190°C and continue to roast for about 1¼ hours, basting the bird regularly with the cooking juices from the bottom of the pan.

Before serving, rest the chicken for 10 minutes.

Carve the chicken into portions, then garnish with the cilantro leaves and serve with the sauce.

In Asia, coconut is used extensively in cooking. It adds a wonderful flavor and texture to so many dishes. Coconut milk is now, luckily, widely available.

Dry Chicken and Coconut Curry

1 lb 2 oz/500 g bite-size chicken pieces on the bone (or, if you don't like bone, diced chicken breasts)

14 fl oz/400 ml canned coconut milk

For the curry paste (or masala, as the Indians call it)

1 inch/2.5 cm piece of fresh gingerroot, peeled and chopped

grated zest of 1 lime

½ teaspoon shrimp paste

6 garlic cloves, peeled and chopped

1 bunch of cilantro leaves (use the stems for this paste and save the leaves for the garnish)

3 shallots, peeled and chopped

1 stem of lemongrass, chopped

2 fresh green chiles, chopped

1 heaped teaspoon mixed caraway and coriander seeds, coarsely crushed in a pestle and mortar

Serves 4–6

Put all the ingredients for the curry paste into a food processor and whiz to a purée.

Heat the coconut milk, then add the chicken pieces and simmer gently until the chicken is tender. If the coconut milk is getting too thick during this process, add a little water.

When the chicken is nearly cooked, stir in the curry paste and continue cooking gently until the chicken is richly coated with the sauce and is really quite dry.

Garnish with the cilantro leaves and serve with any rice and chutneys of your choice (see pages 128–141).

A creamy, rich chicken dish thickened with a walnut paste. Plain rice would be a good accompaniment.

Red Chicken with Walnuts

2 lb 4 oz/1 kg skinned chicken breasts, on the bone

1¾ cups chicken stock

2 tablespoons ghee or clarified butter

1 red onion, peeled and finely chopped

2 garlic cloves, peeled and very finely chopped

1½ tablespoons paprika

1 teaspoon chili powder

1 cup walnuts, finely ground in a food processor

1¼ cups light cream

2 tablespoons walnut oil

salt

a handful of finely shredded flatleaf parsley, to garnish

Serves 4–6

Put the chicken breasts in a pan with the chicken stock, then bring to a boil and simmer for about 15 minutes, or until the chicken is cooked.

Using a slotted spoon, remove the chicken breasts and reserve the stock, then set both aside in a warm place.

Heat the ghee in a pan and cook the onion for a couple of minutes, or until soft but not brown. Add the garlic, 1 tablespoon of the paprika, and the chili powder. Cook for 1 minute more.

Add to this 1 cup of the reserved chicken stock, the walnuts, cream, and salt to taste and heat through, stirring well. If the mixture is a little thick, add a little more of the chicken stock.

Shred the cooked chicken and add to the sauce, stirring it well together, then place on a serving dish.

Gently warm the walnut oil in a small pan and add the remaining paprika, then drizzle over the chicken. Serve garnished with parsley.

The addition of nutmeg to this dish gives it a uniquely savory lift.

18   Chicken Breasts in a Spicy Yogurt Sauce

4 skinned, boneless
chicken breasts

ghee or
clarified butter

2 garlic cloves, peeled
and finely chopped

2 fresh green
chiles, chopped

1 inch/2.5 cm piece
of fresh gingerroot,
peeled and finely
chopped

1 clove, crushed

1¼ cups plain yogurt

*For the masala
(curry paste)*

ghee or
clarified butter

⅓ cup blanched large
almonds, chopped

⅓ cup cashew nuts,
skinned and chopped

2 red onions, peeled
and finely chopped

3–4 fresh green
chiles, chopped

1 teaspoon crushed
poppy seeds

2 bay or
cinnamon leaves

1 teaspoon
nutmeg powder

salt

Serves 4–6

To make the paste, heat some ghee in a skillet and gently cook all the paste ingredients until they are lightly cooked. Add 1 cup of water and simmer for about 10 minutes.

Remove the bay leaves, then put the mixture into a food processor and blend to a smooth paste.

In another pan, heat some ghee, then add the garlic, chiles, ginger, and clove and stir-fry for a minute or so, then add the chicken breasts and cook gently on both sides until they are almost cooked.

Lower the heat and stir in the masala until the chicken pieces are well coated. Add a little water and make sure the mixture is nice and smooth. Gently stir in the yogurt and cook slowly, so as not to curdle the sauce, until the chicken is cooked through.

Although it seems fiddly to eat, chicken left on the bone is the most tasty. Ginger complements chicken (and duck) very well and, despite its simplicity, this is a warming dish, the heat coming from the raw scallion instead of chile.

Ginger Chicken

1 whole free-range chicken, chopped into bite-size pieces on the bone (or, if you are a gastronomic wimp, 4 boneless chicken breasts, cut into bite-size pieces)

vegetable oil, for frying

3 or 4 garlic cloves, peeled and very finely chopped

2 inch/5 cm piece of fresh gingerroot, peeled and grated

1 teaspoon cumin powder

2 teaspoons garam masala powder

juice of 2 lemons or limes

about 1 cup of chicken stock

1 bunch of fiery scallions, finely chopped

salt and freshly ground black pepper

chopped cilantro leaves, to garnish

lemon wedges, to serve

Serves 4–6

Heat some vegetable oil in a skillet and stir-fry the chicken pieces until they are golden, then season with salt and pepper.

Stir in the garlic, ginger, cumin, and garam masala and stir-fry until the pieces are well coated.

Add the lemon juice and chicken stock and simmer gently until the chicken is tender.

At the last minute, add the chopped scallions—they are raw rather than cooked.

Garnish with the cilantro leaves and serve with lemon wedges and saffron rice with cumin (see page 131).

To make this even richer, stir in a little heavy cream just before serving.

These chicken cakes are as good served cold as they are served hot.

Chicken Korma

3 lb/1.4 kg chicken, jointed

scant ⅔ cup ghee or clarified butter

2 large onions, peeled and sliced

1 teaspoon chili powder

4 teaspoons onion powder

1 teaspoon coriander seeds

2 tablespoons cinnamon powder

½ teaspoon ground ginger

10 black peppercorns

5 cloves

6 cardamom pods, ground

2 garlic cloves, peeled and crushed

1 teaspoon salt

1¼ cups plain yogurt

3 bay leaves

1¼ cups chicken stock or water

juice of 1 lemon

Melt the ghee in a large pan and cook the onions until golden brown. Remove from the pan with a slotted spoon and put to one side.

Add all the spices and the garlic to the pan and cook until brown, then throw in the chicken and salt and cook until browned.

Add the yogurt, bay leaves, and stock and return the fried onions to the pan, then bring to a boil. Reduce the heat, then cover with a tight-fitting lid and simmer for 1½–2 hours, or until the chicken is tender.

Remove the pan from the heat, then pour in the lemon juice and mix well. Remove the bay leaves and serve with plain boiled rice.

Serves 4–6

Spicy Chicken Cakes

approx. 1 lb 2 oz/ 500 g ground raw chicken

2 cups bread crumbs

2 fresh green chiles, very finely chopped

3 or 4 tomatoes, skinned, deseeded, and very finely chopped

3 or 4 scallions, very finely chopped

1 large garlic clove, peeled and crushed

1 inch/2.5 cm piece of fresh gingerroot, peeled and finely grated

1 small bunch of cilantro leaves, very finely chopped

a large pinch of cumin powder

1 teaspoon garam masala powder

1 or 2 eggs, beaten

salt and freshly ground black pepper

vegetable oil, for frying

Combine half the bread crumbs with all the other ingredients except the oil, then roll into small balls and flatten to make little cakes.

Press the cakes into the remaining bread crumbs on both sides and shallow-fry in the vegetable oil on both sides until golden.

Serve with any of the salads or chutneys on pages 124–125 and 136–141.

Serves 4–6

Although it may seem strange to cook a savory dish with caramel, this is a popular combination in many parts of Asia. The sweet-savory mixture of the sauce is very delicious.

Spicy Caramelized Chicken Pieces

1 small, free-range chicken, chopped into bite-size pieces on the bone (use the whole chicken)

1 inch/2.5 cm fresh gingerroot, peeled and grated

2 fresh green chiles, finely chopped

salt and freshly ground black pepper

chopped fresh mint, basil, and cilantro leaves, to garnish

For the caramel sauce

generous ½ cup superfine sugar

1 small wine glass of fish sauce

4 or 5 shallots, peeled and very finely diced

Serves 4–6

To make the caramel sauce, melt the sugar gently in a heavy-bottom pan, stirring all the time until it turns brown. Remove from the heat and stir in the fish sauce. Add the shallots, then return to the heat and simmer gently until the sugar has dissolved and you have a smooth, golden sauce. Let cool.

Once the sauce has cooled, add the chicken pieces, ginger, and chiles and simmer gently until the chicken is tender. Season to taste.

Garnish with the fresh herbs and serve with plain boiled rice.

Lemon and chicken are a wonderful combination in this lovely,
fresh-tasting curry. It is not a hot dish, but is full of flavor.

Chicken with Lemon and Turmeric

1 chicken, jointed

**vegetable oil,
for frying**

**2 onions, peeled and
finely chopped**

**4 garlic cloves, peeled
and finely chopped**

**3 tablespoons
turmeric powder**

**1½ teaspoons
cumin powder**

**1½ teaspoons
coriander powder**

**2½ cups fresh
lemon juice**

**6 tomatoes,
skinned, deseeded,
and finely chopped**

**2 cups cooked
chickpeas**

**a good handful
of cilantro leaves,
chopped**

**salt and freshly
ground black pepper**

Serves 4–6

Heat some vegetable oil in a pan and cook the chicken pieces until they
are crisp and golden.

Stir in the onions and garlic and cook until they begin to color, then
season and stir in the turmeric, cumin, and coriander powders. Mix
well to coat the chicken entirely, adding a little more oil if the mixture
is too dry.

Cook the spices gently through for about 5 minutes, stirring so they do
not burn, then add the lemon juice and stir, adding a little water if the
mixture is dry.

Stir in the chopped tomatoes, then season with salt and pepper and
simmer gently for about 1 hour, when you should have a rich sauce.

Add the chickpeas and cilantro leaves and warm through.

Serve with plain yogurt with mint chopped into it.

Pilaf dishes are very popular in Asia. They make meat or poultry go a long way while providing a colorful, spicy, crunchy dish. The addition of saffron really boosts this already delicious recipe.

Chicken Pilaf with Pistachios and Almonds

1 lb/450 g skinned, boneless chicken meat, cut into ½ inch/1 cm cubes

1¾ sticks unsalted butter

⅔ cup blanched almonds, chopped

⅔ cup blanched pistachios, skinned and chopped

2 or 3 fresh red chiles, chopped

generous 2 cups chicken stock

1–1½ cups long-grain rice, washed and strained

a big pinch of saffron threads, soaked in a little hot water

salt and freshly ground black pepper

Serves 4–6

Heat some of the butter in a large skillet and cook the diced chicken until golden.

Add the nuts and chiles and stir-fry for a couple of minutes, then cover with a little of the chicken stock and cook until the chicken is cooked and practically dry. Put to one side.

Melt some more of the butter in another pan and stir-fry the rice until it is well coated with the butter. Add the saffron and its water and the rest of the chicken stock and season with salt and pepper. Bring to a boil, then reduce the heat and simmer gently, covered, for 10–12 minutes.

Add the chicken and nuts and cook gently until the rice has absorbed all the liquid.

Remove the pan from the heat and melt in a few more knobs of unsalted butter, then stir with a fork and let it stand for 4–5 minutes before serving.

This creamy, nutty dish is subtle and mild. Do splash out on a little saffron, as it makes all the difference to the flavor. You should serve the chicken as soon as it is cooked, or the sauce may separate.

Creamy Saffron Chicken

2 lb 4 oz/1 kg chicken breasts, on or off the bone

juice of 1 lemon

⅔ cup cashew nuts

a little milk

8 oz/225 g red onions, peeled and finely sliced

ghee or vegetable oil, for frying

4 garlic cloves, peeled and puréed

1 inch/2.5 cm piece of fresh gingerroot, peeled and puréed

3 inch/7.5 cm cinnamon stick, crushed

5 green cardamom pods, crushed

4 cloves

1¼ cups plain yogurt

a pinch of saffron threads

⅔ cup heavy cream

a handful of cilantro leaves

salt

Serves 4–6

Put the chicken breasts into a bowl, then sprinkle with salt and the lemon juice and let stand in the refrigerator for about 1 hour.

Soak the cashew nuts in the milk for about 1 hour, then purée with the milk in a food processor and put to one side.

Cook the onions in the ghee until completely soft, then add the garlic and ginger purées and stir-fry until the mixture is slightly browned.

In another pan, heat some ghee and cook the cinnamon stick, cardamom pods, and cloves for a couple of minutes, then add the onion paste.

Reduce the heat and stir in the yogurt and saffron, then add the chicken pieces and simmer for 10–15 minutes, or until the chicken is cooked.

Stir in the nut purée and cook for an additional 5 minutes.

At the last minute, stir in the heavy cream and cilantro leaves, then heat through and serve.

There are a lot of chiles in this recipe, but the addition of the cream, yogurt, and nuts means that it will not be too hot.

Pistachio Chicken Curry

2 lb 4 oz/1 kg
boneless chicken
(breasts or thighs), cut
into bite-size pieces

⅔ cup shelled
pistachio nuts

8 fresh green chiles

5 tablespoons
light cream

vegetable oil,
for frying

2 onions, peeled and
finely chopped

1 inch/2.5 cm piece
of fresh gingerroot,
peeled and grated

6 garlic cloves, peeled
and finely chopped

¾ teaspoon garam
masala powder

½ teaspoon
turmeric powder

1 cinnamon stick

¾ teaspoon ground
white pepper

1½ teaspoons
fennel seeds

1 green tomato,
finely chopped

3 tablespoons
plain yogurt

scant 3 cups
chicken stock

salt

For the garnish

1 teaspoon green
cardamom powder

a good handful of
chopped cilantro
leaves

Serves 4–6

Boil the pistachio nuts in a small amount of water for 10 minutes, then drain and cool. When cool, rub off any skin.

Put the pistachios with 4 of the chiles and the light cream into a food processor and whiz to form a paste.

Heat some vegetable oil in a skillet, then add the onions and cook until they are slightly brown. Add the ginger, garlic, garam masala, turmeric, cinnamon, white pepper, and fennel seeds and cook for a couple of minutes.

Add the pistachio mixture and cook for a couple of minutes, then add the chicken and sauté for 5 minutes.

Add the tomato, yogurt, the remaining chiles, and the chicken stock. Add salt to taste and cook for 15–20 minutes, or until the chicken is cooked through.

Just before serving, sprinkle with the cardamom powder and the cilantro leaves.

This is a very simple dish to make, but the use of good, fresh tomatoes and limes, cilantro, and chiles makes it a definite favorite.

Chile and Tomato Chicken

8 chicken thighs, skinned

vegetable oil, for frying

2 shallots, peeled and finely chopped

2 garlic cloves, peeled and chopped

1 lb 2 oz/500 g tomatoes, skinned, deseeded, and finely chopped

1 tablespoon tomato paste

3 fresh red chiles, very finely chopped

2 teaspoons sugar

1½ inch/4 cm piece of fresh gingerroot, peeled and grated

3 teaspoons garam masala powder

1 dessertspoon soy sauce

juice of 2 limes

salt

a handful of cilantro leaves, to garnish

Serves 4–6

Make several cuts in each chicken thigh and put the thighs into an ovenproof dish.

Heat some vegetable oil in a pan and cook the shallots until softened, then add the garlic and cook for about 30 seconds. Add the tomatoes and simmer until you have a rich tomato sauce.

Transfer the tomato sauce to a food processor, and add all the remaining ingredients, except the chicken. Whiz until you have a smooth sauce, then pour the sauce over the chicken and refrigerate for 3 hours to let the chicken absorb the flavors.

Preheat the oven to 375°F/190°C. Put the chicken in the oven and cook, uncovered, for about 1 hour.

Serve hot, garnished with the cilantro leaves, and with a rice dish of your choice (see pages 128–132).

The sharp flavor of lemongrass infuses the chicken, while the slightly caramelized finish gives it an almost sweet and sour flavor. The chile adds zing!

30 Chicken with Lemograss

2 lb/900 g skinned, boneless chicken breast, cut into bite-size pieces

2 garlic cloves, peeled and very finely chopped

1 stem of lemongrass, very finely chopped

2 tablespoons fish sauce

3 tablespoons white sugar

freshly ground black pepper, to taste

vegetable oil, for frying

1 fresh red chile, deseeded and sliced into fine strips

Serves 4–6

Mix together the garlic, lemongrass, fish sauce, 1 tablespoon of the sugar, and some pepper to make a marinade and mix in the chicken pieces. Let stand in the refrigerator for about 1 hour to infuse the flavors.

When the chicken has marinated, heat some vegetable oil in a large pan and sauté the chicken until it is browned on all sides. Cover the pan and simmer over low heat until the chicken is cooked—15–20 minutes.

Heat the remaining sugar in a small pan until it melts and turns a caramel color, but do not let it burn.

Drop in the slivers of chile, then pour onto the chicken and stir to mix.

Serve with plain boiled rice.

In this dish, chicken is cooked in a rich tomato gravy scented with fenugreek leaves and then further enriched with cream and honey.

Chicken livers are often overlooked except for use in terrines. In fact, they have a wonderfully rich flavor and need very little cooking. However, beware: if they are overcooked, they can become bitter. Complemented by the other ingredients, they make this rich, unusual dish.

Spicy Chicken with Tomatoes and Fenugreek

Chilied Chicken Livers with Bell Pepper, Onion, and Tomato

1 lb 12 oz/800 g bone-less chicken, chopped into small pieces

2 lb 4 oz/1 kg ripe tomatoes

4 small red onions, peeled

10 garlic cloves, peeled and 5 finely chopped

1½ inch/4 cm piece of fresh gingerroot, peeled and grated

5 fresh green chiles

5 green cardamom pods

1 teaspoon coriander powder

1 teaspoon cinnamon powder

½ teaspoon mace powder

3 cloves

vegetable oil, for frying

3 tablespoons fenugreek leaves

2 tablespoons ghee or clarified butter

⅔ cup heavy cream

3 tablespoons runny honey

salt and freshly ground black pepper

Serves 4–6

Put the tomatoes, onions, the whole garlic cloves, the ginger, chiles, cardamoms, coriander, cinnamon, mace, and cloves in a large pan with a little water and cook on high heat for about 5 minutes. Cool, then put the lot into a food processor and whiz until you have a smooth, red sauce.

Heat a little vegetable oil in a skillet and cook the chopped garlic until it is just browning, then add the chicken pieces and stir-fry until they are golden.

Pour the tomato sauce in with the chicken and simmer until the chicken is cooked.

Stir in the fenugreek leaves and season.

Just before you serve the dish, stir in the gheer, cream, and honey and heat to warm through.

1 lb/450 g chicken livers, cleaned and trimmed

ghee or clarified butter

2 red onions, peeled and very finely sliced

2 garlic cloves, peeled and crushed

1 red bell pepper, deseeded and finely chopped

1 green bell pepper, deseeded and finely chopped

1 fresh green chile, very finely chopped

½ teaspoon chili powder

3 tomatoes, skinned, deseeded, and finely chopped

salt and freshly ground black pepper

Serves 4–6

Heat some ghee in a large skillet and sauté the onions, garlic, bell peppers, green chile, and chili powder until the vegetables are soft and the chile has released its flavor.

Add the chicken livers and sauté for 5–6 minutes, stirring all the time.

Add the tomatoes and season with salt and pepper. Continue cooking for an additional 2–3 minutes, then serve hot with a bread of your choice (see pages 133–135).

This is a stir-fry dish, as are indeed many curries, which makes it a great quick lunchtime meal. Supermarkets today sell very good curry pastes, and although purists may wish to make their own, bought ones work just as well!

Green Chicken Curry

1 lb/450 g skinned, boneless chicken breasts, cut into pieces

vegetable oil, for frying

3 tablespoons Thai green curry paste

14 fl oz/400 ml canned coconut milk

3 tablespoons fish sauce

1 fresh red chile, deseeded and finely chopped

1 fresh green chile, deseeded and finely chopped

3 tablespoons brown sugar

a handful of fine green beans

a good handful of fresh basil leaves

4 tablespoons coconut cream, to serve

Serves 4–6

Heat some vegetable oil in a large pan or wok and stir in the green curry paste. Cook for about 30 seconds, then throw in the chicken and quickly stir-fry with the paste for a couple of minutes.

Add the coconut milk, fish sauce, chiles, sugar, and beans, then stir well and cook for 5–7 minutes. Toss in the basil leaves.

Serve hot, topped with a dollop of coconut cream.

You could substitute asparagus for the baby leeks if you wish: just prepare them in the same way as the leeks.

This is another typical Thai dish—very light and spicy and very simple. Bird chiles are the very small, very hot chiles. If you prefer, you could substitute larger chiles, cut into very fine strips.

Garlic and Coriander Chicken

4 skinned, boneless chicken breasts

10 baby leeks

vegetable oil

cilantro leaves, to garnish

For the marinade

4 teaspoons coriander seeds

4 teaspoons cumin seeds

5 garlic cloves, peeled and very finely chopped

4 teaspoons paprika

2 teaspoons chili powder

a good grind of black pepper

1 teaspoon salt

2 tablespoons vegetable oil

Serves 4–6

To make the marinade, toast the coriander and cumin seeds in a dry skillet for a few seconds, then grind them in a pestle and mortar. Mix with the rest of the marinade ingredients and stir until well amalgamated.

Cover the chicken breasts with the marinade and put in the refrigerator for 30 minutes.

Brush the leeks with vegetable oil and broil or grill until they are tender.

Grill the chicken on both sides, until golden and cooked through.

Serve the chicken on the baby leeks and garnish with cilantro leaves.

Hot Chicken Salad, Thai Style

8 oz/225 g skinned, cooked chicken

2 tablespoons fish sauce

juice of 1 lime

1 shallot, peeled and finely chopped

2 scallions, finely chopped

a good handful of cilantro leaves, chopped

3 bird chiles, finely ground

fresh mint leaves, to garnish

Serves 4–6

Mix together the chicken, fish sauce, and lime juice.

Add the shallot, scallions, cilantro, and chiles and mix well.

Serve garnished with the mint leaves.

These are great for eating with your fingers. The skin of the squab chickens should be nicely crisp and the meat tender and succulent. This is Indian chicken and chips!

Fried Green Squab Chickens

2 squab chickens, skin on, cut in half along the breastbone and backbone to create halves

juice of 1 lime

vegetable oil

2 potatoes, sliced to a thickness of ½ inch/1 cm

salt

For the masala (curry paste)

6 fresh green chiles

6 garlic cloves, peeled

2 green cardamom pods

1 inch/2.5 cm piece of fresh gingerroot, peeled

2 tablespoons red wine vinegar

2 cloves

1 teaspoon sugar

½ teaspoon cumin seeds

½ teaspoon turmeric powder

juice of ½ lime

1 large bunch of cilantro leaves

Serves 4–6

Pierce the squab chickens all over with a fork, then place in a dish and sprinkle over the lime juice and some salt. Put in the refrigerator for about 30 minutes.

Meanwhile, put all the masala ingredients into a food processor and whiz to form a green paste.

Spread the paste all over the squab chickens and let marinate again in the refrigerator for about 2 hours.

Heat some vegetable oil in a large pan, then add the squab chickens and cook, turning frequently, until they are brown and crispy—about 20 minutes, or until the meat is cooked.

Remove the squab chickens from the pan and set aside to keep warm, leaving the cooking juices in the pan.

Cook the potato slices in the remaining juices until they are golden brown on both sides and serve hot with the squab chickens.

Duck and ginger go very well together. Because it is so fatty, duck retains its flavor through the cooking process; this is a lovely, slightly unusual dish.

Frogs' legs are widely used in Vietnam and, if you are able to obtain them, this recipe makes an interesting change from the French method of cooking them. However, should you feel unable to take this route, chicken wings will work very well.

Curried Duck with Ginger

Frogs' Legs, Vietnamese Style

4 duck joints, skin and fat left on

2 red onions, peeled and thinly sliced

1½ inch/4 cm piece of fresh gingerroot, peeled and cut into fine strips

8–10 garlic cloves, peeled and crushed

2 fresh red chiles, deseeded and cut into fine strips

2 lb 4 oz/1 kg tomatoes, skinned and deseeded

salt and freshly ground black pepper

Serves 4–6

Put the duck joints in a large pan and cover with water. Bring to a boil, then simmer, uncovered, for about 1 hour, or until the water has evaporated and the duck is cooked and sitting in its own fat. Strain off the fat and cover the duck joints with a little more water.

Add the remaining ingredients and simmer for 25–30 minutes, or until the duck is coated in a thick sauce. Season and serve.

1 lb/450 g large frogs' legs

1 small onion, peeled and finely chopped

vegetable oil, for frying

generous ¾ cup coconut milk

1 cup chicken stock

salt and freshly ground black pepper

cilantro leaves, to garnish

For the masala (curry paste)

2 shallots, peeled and finely diced

2 garlic cloves, peeled and finely diced

2 or 3 fresh red chiles, coarsely chopped

1 stem of lemongrass, finely chopped

1 tablespoon curry powder

1 heaped teaspoon brown sugar

a dash of fish sauce

Serves 4–6

Blend all the ingredients for the masala in a food processor until smooth. Cover the frogs' legs with the paste and put to one side.

Sauté the onion in a little vegetable oil until soft, then add the coated frogs' legs and sauté for 2–3 minutes on each side. Season with salt and pepper.

Stir in the coconut milk and simmer gently for about 15 minutes. If it becomes too dry, add a little chicken stock to achieve a smooth sauce.

Garnish with the cilantro leaves and serve with rice or noodles.

Meat Curries

This classic Asian dish makes a great change from good old beef casserole. It is quite hot and dry, but the addition of the coconut milk softens this. It is very delicious served with plain boiled rice.

Beef Rendang

3 lb 5 oz/1.5 kg braising steak, cut into 1 inch/ 2.5 cm cubes

6 dried red chiles, crushed

1 stem of lemongrass, crushed

6 shallots, peeled and finely chopped

3 garlic cloves, peeled and finely chopped

vegetable oil, for frying

1 tablespoon turmeric powder

5–6 Kaffir lime leaves

½ teaspoon tamarind concentrate

juice of 2 limes

14 fl oz/400 ml canned coconut milk

salt and freshly ground black pepper

Serves 4–6

Put the chiles, lemongrass, shallots, and garlic into a food processor and whiz to form a paste.

Heat some vegetable oil in a large casserole and brown the beef. Remove the beef and set aside.

Using the same casserole, cook the paste, stirring all the time, for about 1 minute. Add the turmeric, lime leaves, tamarind concentrate, lime juice, and some black pepper and mix well.

Add the beef and the coconut milk, then cover the pan and cook gently for about 1 hour, or until the beef is cooked and quite dry. Add salt to taste, then serve.

The meatballs are cooked twice—first to brown them all over and then they are simmered in the curry sauce.

The people of Goa add vinegar to lots of their dishes, giving them a distinctive flavor. This is a fairly hot dish—adjust the chiles to your taste.

Curried Meatballs

Goan Beef Curry

1 lb/450 g lean ground beef

2 onions, peeled and finely chopped

4 garlic cloves, peeled and finely chopped

2 teaspoons coriander powder

2 teaspoons chili powder

2 teaspoons turmeric powder

1 teaspoon cumin powder

1 teaspoon ground ginger

1 egg, beaten

vegetable oil, for frying

ghee or clarified butter

salt

a good handful of cilantro leaves, chopped, to garnish

Serves 4–6

Put the beef, half each of the onions, garlic, and spices into a large bowl and add salt to taste, then mix together. Bind the mixture with the beaten egg.

Using your hands, form small meatballs from the beef mixture.

Heat about 1–2 inches/2.5–5 cm of vegetable oil in a pan and gently deep-fry the meatballs for about 5 minutes. Remove from the pan and drain on paper towels.

Heat the ghee in a separate pan and stir-fry the remaining onion and garlic until they have softened, then stir in the remaining spices. Season and stir-fry for 3–4 minutes.

Add the meatballs to this mixture, stirring them around to coat them with the mixture, then add generous ¾ cup of water. Bring to a boil and simmer over low heat for about 30 minutes.

Serve garnished with the chopped cilantro leaves.

2 lb 4 oz/1 kg stewing or braising beef, cut into 1 inch/2.5 cm cubes

vegetable oil, for frying

2 red onions, peeled and finely chopped

2 tomatoes, skinned, deseeded, and finely chopped

4 fresh green chiles, finely chopped

2 tablespoons finely chopped cilantro leaves

4 dried red chiles

10 peppercorns, finely ground in 1 tablespoon vinegar

1 inch/2.5 cm piece of fresh gingerroot, peeled and grated

½ teaspoon cumin seeds

½ teaspoon turmeric powder

salt

Serves 4–6

Heat some vegetable oil in a large skillet and stir-fry the onions, tomatoes, green chiles, and cilantro leaves for 5 minutes.

Add the red chiles, peppercorn mixture, ginger, cumin seeds, and turmeric powder and stir-fry for about 2 minutes.

Add the meat and stir until it is browned. Add about 1 cup of water, then cover the skillet and cook until the meat is tender—about 30 minutes. Season to taste with salt and serve with rice.

Everyone loves roast beef, and this makes a wonderful change
from the norm.

Spiced Roast Beef

4 lb 8 oz/2 kg sirloin of beef	Grind the ginger and garlic together to make a fine paste. Pat the meat dry with paper towels, then prick with a fork and rub in the ginger/garlic paste, lemon juice, and salt to taste. Marinate in the refrigerator for about 6 hours, turning regularly.

**4 lb 8 oz/2 kg
sirloin of beef**

**1 inch/2.5 cm piece
of fresh gingerroot,
peeled**

8 garlic cloves, peeled

**1 tablespoon
lemon juice**

**vegetable oil,
for frying**

10 peppercorns

1 cinnamon stick

8 cloves

6 dried red chiles

**1 tablespoon
Worcestershire sauce**

**1 dessertspoon
cornstarch**

salt

Serves 4–6

Grind the ginger and garlic together to make a fine paste. Pat the meat dry with paper towels, then prick with a fork and rub in the ginger/garlic paste, lemon juice, and salt to taste. Marinate in the refrigerator for about 6 hours, turning regularly.

Preheat the oven to 375°F/190°C. Heat a little vegetable oil in a large oven dish and brown the meat all over. Add 1 cup of water, the peppercorns, cinnamon, cloves, and chiles and roast in the oven for about 2–2½ hours, or until cooked. Remove the meat and put aside to rest.

Mix the Worcestershire sauce with a little water and the cornstarch and stir into the pan juices. Stir over low heat until thickened.

Slice the beef and arrange on a serving dish, then pour the sauce over and serve.

To make tamarind water, cover some tamarind pulp with water and bring to a boil, then let cool. Squeeze out the tamarind and use the water as needed.

Hot-chilied Indonesian Steak

1 lb 5 oz/575 g rump steak, chilled in the refrigerator

2 teaspoons coriander powder

2 tablespoons tamarind water

1 teaspoon brown sugar

8 fresh red chiles, deseeded and finely chopped

4 shallots, peeled and finely chopped

2 garlic cloves, peeled and finely chopped

vegetable oil, for frying

1 teaspoon lemon juice

salt and freshly ground black pepper

Serves 4–6

Using a sharp knife, slice the meat very thinly across the grain and then cut the slices into 2 inch/5 cm squares. Put in a dish in a single layer and sprinkle with the coriander, tamarind water, and sugar and season to taste with salt and pepper. Press the spices down well and let marinate in the refrigerator for about 2 hours.

Put the chiles, shallots, and garlic into a food processor and whiz quickly until fine, but not quite a paste.

Heat some vegetable oil in a pan and cook the meat until browned and cooked through. Using a slotted spoon, remove the meat from the pan and keep it warm.

Add the chile mixture to the remaining oil in the pan and cook, stirring well, for a couple of minutes.

Return the meat to the pan and stir well to coat the meat. Add the lemon juice and serve hot with rice.

This is a hot curry, with a marvellous mix of flavors in it, which work brilliantly together. Best to serve this with a sweet chutney, such as mango (see page 136), and a little plain yogurt.

Hot Drunken Beef

1 lb 9 oz/700 g lean beef, such as sirloin steaks, sliced into thin strips

2 shallots, peeled and finely chopped

1 inch/2.5 cm piece of fresh gingerroot, peeled and finely chopped

2 garlic cloves, peeled and finely chopped

2 Thai chiles, finely chopped

1 fresh red chile, deseeded and sliced lengthwise

1 fresh green chile, deseeded and sliced lengthwise

vegetable oil, for frying

1 teaspoon green peppercorns

4 Kaffir lime leaves, shredded

3½ oz/100 g fine green beans, cut into 1 inch/2.5 cm lengths

1 tablespoon fish sauce

1 teaspoon soft brown sugar

2 teaspoons red wine vinegar

whisky, to flame

a small handful of fresh basil leaves, to garnish

Serves 4–6

Put the shallots, ginger, garlic, and all the chiles into a food processor and whiz to a paste.

Heat a little vegetable oil in a skillet and cook this mixture for about 1 minute. Add the beef, peppercorns, lime leaves, and green beans, then cook for about 5 minutes.

Add the fish sauce, brown sugar, and vinegar and stir well for about 2 minutes.

Pour in the whisky and set alight to flame the dish. When the flames have gone out, garnish with the basil leaves and serve.

The coconut milk provides a rich creamy sauce typical of many
Thai dishes, and is spiced up by the familiar ingredients that go
to make up the curry paste.

Hot Thai Beef Curry

1 lb/450 g braising
steak, sliced thinly
and cut into strips

2 tablespoons
yellow bean sauce

2 tablespoons
Thai red curry paste

4 fresh green chiles,
deseeded and
finely chopped

4 garlic cloves, peeled
and finely chopped

3 shallots, peeled
and finely chopped

1 stem of lemongrass,
finely chopped

1 inch/2.5 cm piece
of fresh gingerroot,
peeled and grated

1 teaspoon
shrimp paste

juice of 1 lime

2 tablespoons
superfine sugar

14 fl oz/400 ml
canned coconut milk

Serves 4–6

Put all the ingredients except the steak and coconut milk into a
food processor and whiz to a paste.

Put the beef and coconut milk in a large pan and bring to a boil.
Cover and simmer for about 40 minutes.

Add the spicy paste and mix thoroughly, then cover and cook for
another 10 minutes.

Serve with your favorite rice (see pages 128–132).

Think "vindaloo" and one tends to think of something dark and hot. An authentic Vindaloo, however, is nothing like that. Gently red in color and brimming with flavor rather than heat, it is a joy.

You can make this dish using just pork, but if you can find fresh eel, do have a go with it. It is delicious.

Pork Vindaloo

Pork and Eel Curry with Red Salad

1 lb 12 oz/800 g pork, diced

vegetable oil, for frying

2 red onions, peeled and finely chopped

4 potatoes, peeled and cut into 1 inch/ 2.5 cm cubes

sugar

salt

For the masala (curry paste)

13–15 dried red chiles

4 fresh green chiles

1 inch/2.5 cm piece of fresh gingerroot, peeled

2 cinnamon sticks

4 cloves

1 teaspoon cumin seeds

1 teaspoon black peppercorns

1 teaspoon turmeric powder

scant ½ cup red wine vinegar

Serves 4–6

Put all the masala ingredients except the vinegar into a food processor and whiz, then add the vinegar to make a smooth paste.

Heat some vegetable oil in a pan and cook the onions until they are soft, then add the masala and stir-fry for a couple of minutes.

Stir in the pork and cook for a couple of minutes, or until the ingredients are all mixed. Add a little water to make a thickish sauce and simmer gently until the meat is nearly cooked.

Add the potatoes, a little sugar, and salt to taste and continue cooking until the potatoes are cooked.

Serve with the rice of your choice (see pages 128–132).

2 lb 4 oz/1 kg shoulder of pork, cubed

1 lb 9 oz/700 g eel, skinned, boned, and cut into pieces

vegetable oil, for frying

2 red onions, peeled and thinly sliced

1 lb 9 oz/700 g tomatoes, skinned, deseeded, and finely chopped

8 garlic cloves, peeled and crushed

2 fresh red chiles, finely chopped

1 inch/2.5 cm piece of fresh gingerroot, peeled and grated

salt

For the red salad

1 red onion, peeled and finely chopped

6 scallions, chopped

3 fresh plum tomatoes, skinned, deseeded, and finely chopped

juice of ½ lime

salt

Serves 4–6

Prepare the red salad by mixing the onions, scallions, and tomatoes together, then sprinkle over the lime juice and season with salt. Put in the refrigerator.

Heat a little vegetable oil in a large pan and cook the pork to seal it without coloring it. Cover with water and simmer for 50 minutes until tender.

Sprinkle the pieces of eel with salt and add to the pan with the onions, tomatoes, garlic, chiles, and ginger. Simmer, uncovered, for about 20 minutes.

Serve with the red salad.

This is a very substantial, peasant-type dish that is highly spiced, but the addition of offal does make it very flavorsome.

Goan Sorpotel

2 lb 4 oz/1 kg boneless pork (leg or shoulder)

1 pig's liver

1 pig's heart

2 pig's kidneys

10 black peppercorns

1 teaspoon cumin seeds

8 cloves

2 cinnamon sticks

12 dried red chiles

10 garlic cloves, peeled

1 inch/2.5 cm piece of fresh gingerroot, peeled

⅔ cup red wine vinegar

vegetable oil, for frying

4 red onions, peeled and finely chopped

6 fresh green chiles, deseeded and finely chopped

salt

Serves 4–6

Put all the meats in a large pan, then cover with water and simmer for about 20 minutes, or until partially cooked. Remove from the pan and dice finely. Reserve the cooking liquid.

Put all the spices and the dried red chiles, garlic, ginger, and vinegar into a food processor and whiz until you have a fine paste.

Heat some vegetable oil in a large pan and gently cook all the meat, stirring continuously, until lightly browned.

Add to this the spice paste and salt to taste and stir-fry for 5 minutes, then add the reserved meat stock, chopped onions, and green chiles.

Lower the heat, then cover the pan and simmer for 45 minutes–1 hour, stirring occasionally, until the sauce has thickened and the oils have risen to the top.

This dish can be served with pappadams or naan bread and the taste improves if it is left overnight and reheated.

Pork really takes up the flavor of any marinade—in this case, soy sauce and pepper. Here, it's then simmered with ginger, onion, and garlic to provide a mildly spiced curry.

Golden Pork

2 lb 4 oz/1 kg shoulder or leg of pork, cut into bite-size pieces

3 tablespoons soy sauce

1½ inch/4 cm piece of fresh gingerroot, peeled—purée half of this, cut the other half into fine strips

2 onions, peeled and puréed

3 garlic cloves, peeled and crushed

1 teaspoon chili powder

vegetable oil, for frying

freshly ground black pepper

Serves 4–6

Put the pork into a bowl with 2 tablespoons of the soy sauce and plenty of black pepper and let marinate for 2 hours in the refrigerator, or 1 hour at room temperature.

Put the puréed ginger, the onions, and garlic into a bowl and pour over a little boiling water. Stir, then strain off and reserve the flavored water and put both to one side.

Stir the chili powder into a little boiling water.

Heat some vegetable oil in a large skillet and quickly stir-fry the strips of ginger, then add the pork and stir-fry until the pork is golden brown.

Add the flavored water and simmer, covered, for about 10 minutes, or until all the liquid is absorbed.

Add the remaining soy sauce, the chili water, and the ginger, onion, and garlic purée. Cover the skillet and cook gently for about 40 minutes, adding a little water if necessary, until the pork is tender.

This is really just a variation on standard meat loaf, but the addition of the fish sauce and chiles really does make a plain dish a little unusual.

Vietnamese Meat Loaf

1 lb 2 oz/500 g
ground pork

1 lb 2 oz/500 g
ground pig's liver

1 cup finely chopped
portobello mushrooms

3 garlic cloves, peeled
and finely chopped

4 shallots, peeled and
finely chopped

2 oz/50 g canned
anchovy fillets in oil,
finely chopped

1 tablespoon
fish sauce

2 fresh red chiles,
deseeded and
finely chopped

freshly ground
black pepper

4 eggs

Serves 4–6

Preheat the oven to 375°F/190°C. Put all the ingredients except the eggs into a large mixing bowl and mix very well together.

Make a well in the middle of the mixture and break in 3 of the eggs, then, using your hands, thoroughly combine the eggs with the pork mixture.

Pack the mixture into a 2 lb/900 g loaf pan, pressing down well. Beat the remaining egg and brush it over the top of the loaf.

Place the loaf pan in a roasting pan of water, so that the water comes about halfway up the sides of the loaf tin, and cover the whole roasting pan with foil. Cook in the oven for about 45 minutes. The loaf is cooked when you prick with a knife and the juices run clear.

Remove from the oven and let cool slightly, then turn out onto a plate.

This dish can be served hot or cold.

The sesame and peanut oils add a lovely flavor to this dish while the turmeric provides color.

Burmese-style Pork

3 lb 5 oz/1.5 kg pork, cubed

1 red onion, peeled

12 garlic cloves, peeled

½ inch/1 cm piece of fresh gingerroot, peeled

8 shallots, peeled

2 tablespoons white wine vinegar

1 tablespoon sesame oil

3 tablespoons peanut oil

2 fresh red chiles, finely chopped

1 teaspoon turmeric powder

1 teaspoon shrimp paste

Serves 4–6

Put the onion, garlic, ginger, shallots, and vinegar into a food processor and whiz together. Transfer to a bowl and mix in the pork. Let marinate in the refrigerator for about 2 hours.

When the pork has marinated, take out the meat, reserving the marinade. Heat the sesame oil and 2 tablespoons of the peanut oil in a large pan and cook the pork, turning until lightly golden all over. Cover with water, then bring to a boil and simmer for 1½ hours.

In another pan, heat the remaining peanut oil, then add the marinade mixture and the chiles and cook for 4–5 minutes. Add the turmeric and shrimp paste and cook for a couple more minutes.

Add this to the cooked pork mixture, stirring well, and simmer for an additional 10 minutes.

The combination of pork and eggplants works very well. When preparing the eggplants, lay the uncooked cubes in a strainer and sprinkle with salt. Let stand for about 10 minutes and you will see they release a lot of liquid. Pat them dry, then fry them. They will keep their texture and flavor better if you do this. The addition of sherry to this dish gives it a distinctly Chinese flavor.

Another great snack food. They can be eaten hot or cold. If you serve them as an entrée, make the balls a little larger.

Pork and Eggplants with Chiles

7 oz/200 g lean pork, cubed

½ inch/1 cm piece of fresh gingerroot, peeled and grated

2 garlic cloves, peeled and chopped

1 tablespoon soy sauce

1 teaspoon dry sherry

vegetable oil, for frying

8 oz/225 g eggplant, cubed (see above)

2 fresh red chiles, finely chopped

4 tablespoons chicken stock

salt

2 scallions, finely chopped, to garnish

Put the pork, ginger, garlic, soy sauce, and sherry into a large bowl and mix together, then let stand in the refrigerator for 30 minutes.

Heat some vegetable oil in a heavy-bottomed pan and fry the eggplant until golden. Remove and drain on paper towels.

In the same pan, cook the pork mixture, turning frequently, for about 2 minutes, then add the eggplant and chiles and cook for an additional 2 minutes.

Add the stock, then cover and cook until nearly all the liquid has gone. Add salt to taste and serve hot, garnished with the chopped scallions.

Serves 4–6

Pork Balls with Lemongrass

1 lb/450 g lean ground pork

4 stems of lemongrass, very finely chopped

½ inch/1 cm piece of fresh gingerroot, peeled and grated

2 tomatoes, skinned, deseeded, and finely chopped

1 teaspoon turmeric powder

juice of ½ lime

2 tablespoons Thai red curry paste

vegetable oil, for frying

Put all the ingredients except the vegetable oil into a large bowl and mix together. Then, using your hands, form the mixture into small balls.

Fry the pork balls in about 1 inch/ 2.5 cm of hot oil for 4–5 minutes, or until golden brown. Remove with a slotted spoon and drain on paper towels.

Serve by themselves as a snack or with rice.

Serves 4–6

This is a one-pot dish that just needs rice and a relish to accompany it.
You could also make it with chicken instead of lamb. This recipe will
need to be started the day before.

Lamb Dhansak

1 lb 2 oz/500 g
stewing lamb or
mutton, cut
into cubes

1 lb 2 oz/500 g
yellow lentils

generous ½ cup
red lentils

⅔ cup mung beans,
soaked overnight

oil or ghee, for frying

2 red onions,
peeled and
finely sliced

½ teaspoon
turmeric powder

1 teaspoon
coriander powder

1 teaspoon
cumin powder

1 eggplant, peeled
and diced

9 oz/250 g pumpkin,
peeled and diced

salt

1 lb 2 oz/500 g fresh
spinach leaves, well
washed and drained

*For the masala
(curry paste)*

6–8 garlic cloves,
peeled

2 inch/5 cm piece of
fresh gingerroot,
peeled and chopped

6–8 dried red chiles

6 green
cardamom pods

1 cinnamon stick

½ teaspoon black
peppercorns

1 tablespoon
coriander seeds

1 tablespoon
cumin seeds

Serves 4–6

Rinse and drain the lentils and mung beans. Grind all the masala
ingredients with a little water to make a smooth paste.

Heat the oil and cook the onions until golden brown, then stir in the
masala paste, turmeric, coriander, and cumin and stir-fry gently for
about 5 minutes.

Stir in the lamb and cook gently over low heat until the meat is coated
with the masala paste and any liquid from the meat has been absorbed.
The dish should be quite dry.

Add the lentils, peas, eggplant, and pumpkin and stir in a little water
to form a gravy. Season with salt. Bring to a boil, then reduce the heat
and simmer gently, covered, for about 30 minutes, or until the meat
is cooked.

Remove the meat from the pan and put to one side. Purée the lentils,
vegetables and gravy in a food processor and return the meat to
this mixture.

Quickly stir-fry the spinach in hot oil, then add to the lamb mixture
and serve.

This may sound a little strange, but cooking in milk is, in fact, commonplace in parts of Asia and makes for a nice, subtle, pale curry.

Kashmiri Lamb in Milk

750 g/1 lb 10 oz lamb chops

9 oz/250 g lamb bones, for stock

a pinch of saffron

vegetable oil, for frying

2 red onions, peeled and finely grated

2 cloves

2 cinnamon sticks

5 green cardamom pods

scant 5 cups milk

2 tablespoons light cream

1 teaspoon fennel powder

½ teaspoon cumin powder

½ teaspoon ground white pepper

½ teaspoon sugar

1 fresh green chile, deseeded and finely sliced

salt and freshly ground black pepper

Serves 4–6

Soak the saffron in 2 tablespoons of water.

Heat a little vegetable oil in a pan and cook the onions until soft and golden.

Put the lamb chops and bones in a large pan with about 2½ cups of water, 1 clove, 1 cinnamon stick, 3 cardamom pods, the onions, and a pinch of salt. Bring to a boil, then cover the pan and simmer for about 15–20 minutes, or until the meat is tender. Strain and reserve the stock, keeping the chops but discarding the bones.

Pour the milk into another pan and add the remaining clove, cinnamon stick, and cardamom pods. Bring to a boil, stirring gently, and cook until the milk reduces by about a third. Take off the heat and strain, then pour back into the pan. Set aside until cool, then stir in the cream.

Add the chops and about 1¼ cups of the stock to the spiced milk and warm over low heat.

Heat a little more oil in a skillet and add the fennel and cumin powders and the white pepper and cook for a few seconds. Add this to the chops and stock mixture, and stir in the sugar. Season to taste.

Add the chile and the saffron to the lamb mixture and simmer for 2–3 minutes, then serve with rice.

The cilantro-flavored yogurt tenderizes this lamb dish and lying in wait for the unwary are whole green chiles stuffed with a fennel, mustard, cumin, and fenugreek mixture.

Pickling-spiced Lamb

1 lb 12 oz/800 g shoulder or leg of lamb, cut into bite-size pieces

2 good handfuls of cilantro leaves

scant 1¼ cups plain yogurt

2 red onions, peeled and chopped

2 garlic cloves, peeled

1 inch/2.5 cm piece of fresh gingerroot, peeled

1 heaped teaspoon fennel seeds

1 teaspoon mustard seeds

1 teaspoon cumin seeds

1 teaspoon fenugreek seeds

8 fresh green chiles

vegetable oil, for frying

½ teaspoon turmeric powder

salt

Put the cilantro leaves and yogurt into a food processor and whiz together. Tip into a bowl and set aside.

Put the onions, garlic, and ginger into the food processor and whiz together, then set aside.

Grind together the fennel, mustard, cumin, and fenugreek seeds. Slit the green chiles down one side and remove the seeds to create a pocket, then stuff the pocket with half of the spice mixture. Reserve the rest.

Heat some vegetable oil in a large pan and cook the stuffed chiles for a couple of minutes. Add the puréed onion mixture and cook gently for about 10 minutes.

Add the reserved spices and stir for about 1 minute, then add the yogurt mix, turmeric powder, and some salt. Bring to a boil, then add the meat and mix well.

Turn down the heat, then cover the pan and simmer until the meat is tender, 45 minutes–1 hour.

Serve with Saffron Rice with Cumin (see page 131).

Serves 4–6

Lamb chops are coated in a creamy marinade and left for about 5 hours at room temperature, longer if they are in the refrigerator. You could serve these with a vegetable curry and rice.

This dish is quite dry when cooked, but it is full of flavor. Served in pitta bread with yogurt, it makes a great snack meal.

Spicy Lamb Chops

Curried Lamb with Cilantro

8 thick lamb chops, trimmed of fat

a good handful of unsalted cashew nuts

1¾ cups milk

a little vegetable oil

2 teaspoons ground white pepper

3 garlic cloves, peeled

1 inch/2.5 cm piece of fresh gingerroot, peeled

1¾ cups plain yogurt

4 fresh green chiles, finely chopped

2 teaspoons mixed mace, nutmeg, and cardamom powder

1 teaspoon ground ginger

salt

Serves 4–6

Soak the cashew nuts in the milk for about 30 minutes, then drain and liquidize to form a paste. Set this aside.

Meanwhile, place the chops in an ovenproof dish and rub with vegetable oil, the white pepper, and some salt and put in the refrigerator for 10–15 minutes. Grind the garlic and ginger together into a paste.

Put the yogurt, cashew nut paste, chiles, ginger and garlic paste, mixed mace, nutmeg, and cardamom powder, ground ginger, and salt into a food processor and whiz until you have a creamy marinade.

Pour over the chops and let stand for about 5 hours, longer if you put them in the refrigerator.

Preheat the oven to 425°F/220°C. Place the chops on a trivet in a roasting pan and roast in the oven for 10 minutes, then turn and roast for an additional 10 minutes.

Finally, finish the chops off under a hot broiler for a couple of minutes on both sides to fully brown them.

750 g/1 lb 10 oz ground lamb

vegetable oil, for frying

2 medium red onions, peeled and finely chopped

5 garlic cloves, peeled and finely chopped

½ inch/1 cm piece of fresh gingerroot, peeled and grated

2 fresh green chiles, finely chopped

3 cloves

3 green cardamom pods, crushed

¼ teaspoon turmeric powder

1½ teaspoons coriander powder

1 teaspoon cumin powder

1 teaspoon garam masala powder

2 tomatoes, finely chopped

1 cinnamon stick

a good handful of chopped cilantro leaves

salt

Serves 4–6

Heat a little vegetable oil in a pan and cook the onions until they are golden.

Add the garlic, ginger, and chiles and cook for a couple of minutes, then add the lamb and cook for about 5 minutes.

Add the cloves, cardamom pods, turmeric, coriander, cumin, and half the garam masala powders and cook, stirring, for another few minutes. Add the tomatoes and cinnamon stick and season to taste.

When the tomatoes are cooked, add a couple of cups of water and continue to cook for about 30 minutes, or until the lamb is cooked and tender.

Add the chopped cilantro and the remaining garam masala and cook for a few more minutes until you have a fairly dry consistency.

Serve with pita bread and plain yogurt.

Ground almonds enrich this smooth gravy, in which is simmered lamb
or mutton. You can buy rose water in most chemist stores.

Rogan Josh

1 lb 12 oz/800 g
lamb or mutton, cut
into bite-size pieces

1 cup
plain yogurt

scant ½ cup
tomato paste

1 tablespoon
ground almonds

salt

*For the masala
(curry paste)*

vegetable oil,
for frying

4 cardamom pods

4 cloves

4 tablespoons ginger
and garlic purée (just
take equal quantities
of peeled garlic and
fresh gingerroot and
purée together)

1 teaspoon
chili powder

2 tablespoons brown
onion paste (sauté
finely diced red
onions in oil until
golden brown,
then purée)

½ tablespoon garam
masala powder

For the garnish

chopped cilantro
leaves

1 inch/2.5 cm piece
of fresh gingerroot,
peeled and cut into
thin strips

a good pinch of
saffron threads,
soaked in
3 tablespoons
rose water

Serves 4–6

To make the masala, heat some oil, then add the cardamom pods
and cloves and cook until they crackle. Add the rest of the masala
ingredients and stir-fry for a minute or so.

Stir in the lamb and yogurt, then season with salt and stir-fry for
3–4 minutes to coat the lamb with the yogurt and masala. Add a
little water and simmer gently for about 45 minutes to 1 hour, or until
the lamb is almost tender.

Mix in the tomato paste and continue cooking until the liquid is
reduced by about one-third. Stir in the ground almonds.

Turn out into a serving dish and garnish with the cilantro leaves and
ginger strips, then sprinkle on the saffron and rose water and serve.

This must be cooked in a very hot oven to achieve that authentic tandoori appearance and flavor. The addition of melted butter at the end gives it additional richness.

Tandoori Lamb

4 small racks of lamb

2 tablespoons melted butter

For the marinade

1¼ cups plain yogurt

3 tablespoons heavy cream

1 egg yolk

6 garlic cloves, peeled and finely chopped

1 inch/2.5 cm piece of fresh gingerroot, peeled and grated

juice of 1 lime

2 teaspoons chili powder

2 teaspoons garam masala powder

1 teaspoon turmeric powder

a small handful of cilantro leaves

1 teaspoon freshly ground black pepper

salt

Serves 4–6

To make the marinade, mix together the yogurt, cream, and egg yolk in a small bowl.

Put the garlic, ginger, lime juice, and some salt into a food processor and whiz together, then stir into the yogurt mixture. Add all the other marinade ingredients and stir well.

Remove any skin from the lamb and prick holes all over the meat. Rub the marinade well into the lamb, then cover and let stand in the refrigerator, preferably overnight.

Preheat the oven to 425°F/220°C. Roast the lamb in the oven for 20–25 minutes, or longer if you do not like your meat too rare.

When the lamb is cooked, remove from the oven and brush all over with the melted butter, then return to the oven for 2–3 minutes more.

Slice and serve with a salad.

Marinated lamb is served in a creamy, aromatic sauce. Try it with Saffron Rice with Cumin (see page 131).

Lamb in Spiced Sauce

1 lb 2 oz/500 g lamb, cut into bite-size pieces

1 inch/2.5 cm piece of fresh gingerroot, peeled and grated

3 garlic cloves, peeled and crushed

vegetable oil, for frying

2 blades mace

10 green cardamom pods

4 black cardamom pods

10 cloves

3 bay leaves

2 red onions, peeled and finely diced

½ teaspoon turmeric powder

½ teaspoon chili powder

1 teaspoon coriander powder

⅔ cup tomato paste

¼ cup heavy cream

salt

Serves 4–6

Purée together the ginger and garlic and use half of it to spread on the lamb, then let stand for 1 hour for the flavors to infuse.

Heat some vegetable oil in a pan and cook the mace, green and black cardamom pods, cloves, and bay leaves until they crackle, then add the onions and stir-fry until they are golden brown.

Add the rest of the garlic and ginger paste and all the other spices, then season with salt and cook for a few minutes.

Stir in the lamb and cook until sealed. Add a little water, then cover the pan and simmer the lamb for about 45 minutes to 1 hour, or until tender.

When the lamb is cooked, remove from the juices and set aside. Pour the sauce into a food processor and whiz until smooth. Strain it into another pan and gently reheat, then add the tomato paste and simmer until it is rich and thick. Lower the heat and stir in the cream, then season and place the lamb in the sauce to reheat. Serve hot.

This is a dish for a special occasion. Succulent lamb is combined with fragrant rice and decorated with nuts, herbs, and ghee.

Lamb Biryani

4 lb 8 oz/2 kg lamb, cut into bite-size pieces

4 garlic cloves, peeled

1 inch/2.5 cm piece of fresh gingerroot, peeled

2 teaspoons chili powder

ghee or clarified butter

2 red onions, peeled and finely chopped

1 cup slivered almonds

scant 1¼ cups plain yogurt

2 lb 4 oz/1 kg basmati rice, thoroughly washed in cold water, then drained and soaked in fresh water for 1 hour

scant ½ cup heavy cream

100 g/3½ oz golden raisins

generous ½ cup cashew nuts

a large handful of fresh mint leaves, chopped

a large handful of cilantro leaves, chopped

a few drops of rose water (see page 61)

a pinch of saffron threads, soaked in 2 tablespoons water

juice of 1 large lemon

salt

For the masala (curry paste)

10 cardamom pods

10 cloves

4 blades mace

1 teaspoon cinnamon powder

Serves 4–6

Roast the spices for the masala in a dry pan for a few seconds, then grind them and put to one side.

Purée the garlic and ginger together and mix in the chili powder.

Heat some ghee in a large pan and stir-fry the onions until they are soft and slightly browned, then stir in the masala powder and the garlic and ginger purée and cook for about 5 minutes, stirring all the time.

Stir in half the slivered almonds and add the lamb, then stir in the yogurt and a little water. Cover the pan and cook for about 1 hour, or until the lamb is tender.

Meanwhile, drain the rice thoroughly. Heat some ghee in a large skillet and sauté the rice for about 3 minutes, making sure all the grains are coated in the fat.

Add enough water to just cover the rice, then season and cook gently over low heat until the rice is cooked and the water has evaporated. Set aside and keep the rice warm.

Stir the cream into the lamb and continue to cook gently to warm through. Sprinkle in half the golden raisins, half the cashew nuts, and half the chopped herbs and pour the lamb into a serving dish.

Mix the rest of the golden raisins, cashew nuts, and herbs, and the rose water, saffron, and lemon juice with the rice and spoon the rice evenly over the lamb.

Toast the remaining slivered almonds in a dry pan and sprinkle them over the dish along with some melted ghee.

This is a substantial curry, needing little more than some naan bread (see page 133). You can ask your butcher to chop up the lamb for you.

The vinegar, sugar, and apricots give this curry a slightly sweet piquancy. If you're short of time, you could use no-soak, soft, dried apricots.

Curried Lamb with Green Peas

Lamb Curry with Apricots

2 lb 4 oz/1 kg lamb shank, cut into steaks across the bone

vegetable oil, for frying

3 onions, peeled and finely chopped

1 tablespoon red masala curry paste

1 star anise

5 fresh green chiles, chopped

5 garlic cloves, peeled and finely chopped

a few sprigs of fresh thyme

4 cups chicken or lamb stock

1 lb/450 g potatoes, cut into small cubes

4 cups frozen peas

salt and freshly ground black pepper

Serves 4–6

Heat some vegetable oil in a large skillet and brown the lamb steaks.

Add the onions and cook until they are softened, then add the curry paste, star anise, chiles, garlic, and thyme.

Pour in the stock, then cover and cook for 20 minutes.

Add the potatoes and cook for another 20 minutes, or until the potatoes are cooked.

Add the peas, then bring back to a simmer and cook for 5–10 minutes. Season to taste and serve.

1 lb 10 oz/750 g stewing lamb, cut into bite-size pieces

vegetable oil, for frying

2 red onions, peeled and very finely chopped

½ inch/1 cm piece of fresh gingerroot, peeled and grated

4 garlic cloves, peeled and crushed

1 cinnamon stick

4 green cardamom pods, lightly crushed

1½ teaspoons chili powder

2 teaspoons cumin powder

3 tomatoes, skinned, deseeded, and finely chopped

¾ teaspoon garam masala powder

1 teaspoon red wine vinegar

1 teaspoon sugar

scant ⅔ cup dried apricots, soaked in water for 3 hours to soften

salt and freshly ground black pepper

Serves 4–6

Heat some vegetable oil in a large skillet and stir-fry the onions until they are golden.

Add the ginger and garlic and cook for a couple more minutes.

Add the cinnamon stick and cardamom pods and cook for a minute, then add the chili and cumin powders and stir well to amalgamate.

Add the tomatoes and cook for 5–6 minutes, then add the meat, garam masala, and black pepper to taste and stir-fry for 5–7 minutes.

Season with salt, then cover the skillet and cook slowly over low heat for about 45 minutes to 1 hour, or until tender.

At the last minute stir in the vinegar, sugar, and apricots and heat through, stirring well.

Fish Curries

Amazingly, carrots and shrimp do go together. With the lemongrass, mint, chiles, lemon juice, and lime leaves, this soup is very light and very quick to make.

Spicy Carrot and Shrimp Soup

12 large raw shrimp, shelled and deveined (see page 72)

generous 2 cups fresh carrot juice

1 tablespoon finely chopped lemongrass

2 or 3 fresh red chiles, finely chopped

4 or 5 fresh or dried Kaffir lime leaves, finely chopped

1 small bunch of cilantro leaves, finely chopped

1 small bunch of fresh mint leaves, finely chopped

a dash of fish sauce

juice of 1 lime or 1 lemon

salt and freshly ground black pepper

1 stick butter, melted, to serve

chopped cilantro leaves, to garnish

Serves 4–6

Heat the carrot juice in a pan with the lemongrass, chiles, lime leaves, cilantro, and mint and simmer gently for about 5 minutes.

Add the fish sauce, lime juice, and salt and pepper to taste, then add the shrimp and cook for an additional 2–3 minutes, or until the shrimp have turned pink.

Serve into bowls and top each bowl with some melted butter and chopped cilantro.

Good-quality, large shrimp have plenty of flavor, but do buy raw shrimp. You will know they are cooked when they turn pink. The spices in this dish add just the right amount of color and flavor.

It is another easy, yet impressive curry. Serve with either plain or dill rice (see page 128).

Burmese Shrimp Curry

1 lb 4 oz/550 g large raw shrimp, shelled and deveined (see page 72)

2 tablespoons soy sauce

a dash of fish sauce

½ teaspoon turmeric powder

vegetable oil, for frying

1 large onion, peeled and chopped

4 garlic cloves, peeled and finely chopped

½ teaspoon chili powder

1 fresh green chile, deseeded and finely chopped

1 inch/2.5 cm piece of fresh gingerroot, peeled and grated

4 tomatoes, chopped

a handful of chopped cilantro leaves, plus whole leaves to garnish

salt

Serves 4–6

Put the shrimp into a bowl with the soy sauce, fish sauce, turmeric, and a little salt, then mix well together and let stand in the refrigerator for 30 minutes.

Heat a little vegetable oil in a skillet and cook the onion, garlic, and chili powder for a couple of minutes.

Next, add the shrimp, fresh chile, ginger, tomatoes, and chopped cilantro and cook for 5 minutes.

Add a small amount of water and simmer, covered, for 10–15 minutes, or until the sauce is quite thick.

Serve garnished with cilantro leaves.

Chickpeas are grown extensively in India, where they form an important part of the diet for vegetarians. Here they are added to rice and shrimp for a meal in one.

Shrimp with Rice and Chickpeas

20 large raw shrimp, shell on

vegetable oil, for frying

1 onion, peeled and finely chopped

4 garlic cloves, peeled and crushed

1½ teaspoons cardamom powder

1 teaspoon cumin powder

5 fresh red chiles, deseeded and finely chopped

generous 2 cups short-grain rice, washed and drained

4 tomatoes, skinned, deseeded, and finely chopped

4 cups chicken stock

11 oz/300 g cooked chickpeas

juice of 2 lemons

salt and freshly ground black pepper

cilantro leaves, to garnish

Serves 4–6

Remove the heads and shells of the shrimp, leaving the tails on, and cut a slit down the back of each one. Take out and discard the black vein that runs through the shrimp. Set the shrimp aside.

Heat some vegetable oil in a large skillet and cook the onion and garlic until browned, then add the cardamom, cumin, and chiles and cook for a few minutes.

Stir in the rice until it is thoroughly mixed with the other ingredients, then stir in the tomatoes and add enough of the chicken stock to cover. Season, then stir once and put on a lid. Cook on low heat for about 20 minutes, or until all the liquid has been absorbed.

Stir in the chickpeas and set aside to keep warm.

In another pan, heat some oil and quickly stir-fry the shrimp until they turn pink. Stir in the lemon juice, then season with salt and pepper and mix the shrimp into the rice and chickpeas.

Serve sprinkled with the cilantro.

These two ingredie
hot dish, so may a
get fresh pineapple

Curried Sh

14 oz/400 g co
shelled sh

1 fresh red
finely cho

1 fresh green
finely cho

10 shallots, p
and finely cho

10 blanched alm
cho

1 stem of lemong
cho

1 inch/2.5 cm
of fresh ginge
peeled and g

a little gh
vegetab
for

14 fl oz/40
canned coconu

1 sma
pineapple, p
cored, ar
into

a dash of fish

a hand
cilantro

Serve

Fresh curry le
fresh leaves, y
Asian food sto

Hot, Sw

11 oz/3
shrimp
and
(see

1½ t
tama

5 fresh gre
finely

3 garlic clove
and finely

1
cur

vege

2 large onion
and finely

¾
coriand

½
cum

½
ch

1 teasp
masa

½
turmer

Colorful, healthy, and quick, quick, quick!

You must use large, whole shrimp for this dish to appreciate their flavor.

Stir-fried Shrimp and Spinach

Shrimp Kabobs

1 lb 2 oz/500 g large raw shrimp, peeled and deveined (see page 72)

a dollop of ghee or clarified butter, for frying

3 garlic cloves, peeled and finely chopped

1 large onion, peeled and finely chopped

1 teaspoon garam masala powder

1 teaspoon coriander powder

1 teaspoon turmeric powder

a pinch of chili powder, or to taste

a pinch of ground ginger, or to taste

1 tablespoon tomato paste

1 lb/450 g fresh spinach leaves, washed and drained

Serves 4–6

Heat the ghee in a large skillet, then add the garlic and onion and cook gently until soft.

Add the spices and tomato paste and stir-fry for 4–5 minutes, then stir in the spinach leaves until they soften.

Add the shrimp and stir-fry until they have turned pink and are coated with the softened spinach, spices, and the sauce. Serve at once.

3 or 4 large, raw shrimp, heads and shells removed, tails left on, per person

For the marinade

2½ cups of plain yogurt

2 garlic cloves, peeled and crushed

2 teaspoons garam masala powder

2 heaped teaspoons coriander powder

salt and freshly ground black pepper

For the garnish

chopped cilantro leaves

1 crunchy scallion, cut in half and finely sliced lengthwise

1 or 2 fresh green chiles, finely chopped

½ lime per person, to serve

Serves 4–6

Mix together all the ingredients for the marinade. Devein the shrimp (see page 72) and thread them onto skewers. Put in a dish, then cover with the marinade and let stand in the refrigerator for 2–3 hours.

Preheat the broiler or grill, then put the kabobs on a rack and cook for about 5 minutes, turning from time to time. If there is any marinade mixture left, use a pastry brush to baste the skewers with the mixture.

Once the kabobs are plated, sprinkle the garnish over them and serve with lime halves.

As with other recipes, do not overcook the shrimp and squid.
They literally take only a couple of minutes.

Squid and Shrimp in Turmeric Gravy

7 oz/200 g squid, cut into squares and scored over the surface

11 oz/300 g raw shrimp, shelled and deveined (see page 72)

1 small zucchini, cut into strips and blanched in boiling water for 1 minute

1 cup fine green beans, blanched in boiling water for 1 minute

1 large fresh red chile, deseeded and cut into fine strips

1 large fresh green chile, deseeded and cut into fine strips

14 fl oz/400 ml canned coconut milk

salt and freshly ground black pepper

For the turmeric gravy

10 large fresh red chiles, deseeded and chopped

5 shallots, peeled and finely chopped

1 inch/2.5 cm piece of fresh gingerroot, peeled and grated

1 tablespoon turmeric powder

vegetable oil, for frying

¼ cup tamarind water (see page 44)

1 cup fish stock

Serves 4–6

To prepare the turmeric gravy, put the chiles, shallots, ginger, and turmeric into a food processor and whiz until smooth.

Heat a little vegetable oil in a skillet and add the paste. Stir-fry for about 4 minutes, then add the tamarind water and fish stock.

Bring to a boil and simmer for 10 minutes, or until the gravy thickens a little.

Add the squid and shrimp, the vegetables and chiles and simmer for a couple of minutes, then add the coconut milk and stir over the heat for another couple of minutes to heat through. Season with salt and pepper to taste, then serve.

This dish is quite hot—there are a lot of chiles in there! You could use less if you wish, but if you have the stamina, be brave and follow the recipe. It will be really tangy.

Bream in Ginger, Chile, and Tomato

4 good-size
bream fillets

1 teaspoon salt

a pinch of freshly
ground black pepper

a good handful
of cilantro leaves,
chopped

vegetable oil, for frying

8 cherry tomatoes

4 Thai chiles,
left whole

8 sprigs of lemon basil

For the sauce

vegetable oil, for frying

10 fresh red chiles,
deseeded and finely
chopped

8 garlic cloves, peeled
and finely chopped

1½ inch/4 cm piece
of fresh gingerroot,
peeled and grated

2 stems of
lemongrass, crushed

2 Kaffir lime
leaves, torn

salt

Serves 4–6

To prepare the sauce, heat some vegetable oil in a skillet and add the chiles, garlic, and ginger. Stir-fry over low heat for about 3 minutes to release the flavors.

Add the lemongrass, lime leaves, salt to taste, and generous 1½ cups of water and simmer for about 10 minutes.

Remove the lemongrass and lime leaves and whiz the sauce in a food processor until smooth. Set aside.

Season the bream fillets with the salt, pepper, and cilantro leaves.

In another pan, heat some oil and flash-fry the fish on both sides for 2 minutes a side.

Add the tomatoes and cook for 30 seconds, then add the prepared sauce and the whole Thai chiles. Simmer for a couple of minutes, then add the basil sprigs and serve.

Steaming fish does help to keep its texture and flavor, and it also
preserves the flavor of the spices.

Steamed Fish Curry

1 lb/450 g firm white
fish fillets (see page
85), thinly sliced

a good handful of
spinach leaves

a few sprigs of
fresh basil

a few sprigs of
fresh mint

2 eggs, beaten

14 fl oz/400 ml
canned coconut milk

2 tablespoons
fish sauce

3 tablespoons Thai
red curry paste

1 fresh red chile,
deseeded and
finely chopped

1 fresh green chile,
deseeded and
finely chopped

a good handful of
cilantro leaves,
chopped

4 Kaffir lime
leaves, torn

Serves 4–6

Using a dish that will fit in a steamer, line the dish with the spinach,
basil, and mint leaves.

Mix together the eggs, coconut milk, fish sauce, and curry paste and
stir well. Fold the fish slices into this and pour into the lined dish.

Sprinkle the chiles, cilantro, and lime leaves on top, then cover and
steam for 15–20 minutes.

Serve with rice of your choice (see pages 128–132).

This is an unusual dish—the fish is marinated and then fried before being cooked in a rich, red sauce in the oven.

Egyptian Fish Curry

2 lb/900 g firm white fish fillets (see page 85), cut into 1½ inch/4 cm squares

olive oil

juice of 1 lemon

2 pinches of saffron strands

vegetable oil, for frying

2 onions, peeled and coarsely chopped

3–4 garlic cloves, peeled and crushed

2 green bell peppers, deseeded and coarsely chopped

1¾ cups tomato passata (tomato sauce from a jar or can)

3 bird chiles, crumbled

1 teaspoon cumin powder

seasoned flour

salt and freshly ground black pepper

Serves 4–6

Marinate the fish in enough olive oil to coat it lightly, the lemon juice, and 1 pinch of the saffron strands for about 40 minutes.

Heat some vegetable oil in a skillet and cook the onions, garlic, and green bell peppers until they are nearly cooked, but still have texture.

Add the tomato passata, chiles, cumin, and the remaining saffron, then season with salt and pepper and cook until the sauce has reduced by about a fifth, has thickened, and is rich red in color.

Remove the fish from the marinade and dry on paper towels, then dredge in the seasoned flour and cook on both sides in hot oil until golden on the outside.

Preheat the oven to 400°F/200°C. Put half the tomato sauce in the bottom of a shallow ovenproof dish, then layer the fish pieces on top and cover with the remaining sauce.

Bake in the oven for about 15 minutes, then serve.

This is quick and easy to make and is ideal for lunch or a swift snack.

The vegetables in this dish are steamed to keep their texture. It is a light, simple, and healthy dish that should appeal to everyone.

Hot Fish Balls with Cucumber Relish

Hot and Sour Fish

1 lb 10 oz/750 g white fish fillets, skinned, washed, and cubed

2 garlic cloves, peeled

a large handful of cilantro leaves

18–20 mixed peppercorns

3 dried red chiles, crumbled

½ teaspoon superfine sugar

1 tablespoon all-purpose flour

1 tablespoon soy sauce

vegetable oil, for deep-frying

For the cucumber relish

½ cucumber, peeled, deseeded, and finely chopped

2 shallots, peeled and very finely chopped

1 small carrot, very finely chopped

1 teaspoon red wine vinegar

1 teaspoon sugar

Serves 4–6

To make the relish, mix together all the ingredients and set aside in the refrigerator.

Put the garlic, cilantro, peppercorns, chiles, and sugar into a food processor and whiz to a paste.

Add the fish to the paste and whiz in the food processor until smooth, then add the flour and soy sauce and whiz again to combine.

Using your hands, shape the mixture into golf-ball-size balls.

Heat about 1½ inches/4 cm of vegetable oil in a skillet and deep-fry the fish balls until they are golden. Remove from the pan and drain on paper towels.

Serve hot with the cucumber relish.

1 lb/450 g firm, white fish fillets (see page 85)

vegetable oil, for deep-frying

2 garlic cloves, peeled and finely chopped

8 oz/225 g okra, chopped into ½ inch/ 1 cm pieces

8 oz/225 g tomatoes, cut into fourths

2 fresh red chiles, deseeded and finely chopped

1 small can of pineapple chunks in juice

a few slices of white radish

1 onion, peeled, finely sliced, and fried until crisp

5 or 6 fresh curry leaves

a good handful of fresh basil leaves

Serves 4–6

Heat about 1 inch/2.5 cm of vegetable oil in a deep pan and fry the fish fillets and garlic in batches for 3–4 minutes. Do not overcrowd the pan. Drain and keep in a warm place.

Steam the okra, tomatoes, chiles, pineapple, and radish for about 5 minutes to keep their texture and put on a serving dish.

Lay the fish fillets over the vegetables and sprinkle on the fried onions, curry leaves, and basil leaves.

If you can't find banana leaves (Asian stores sell them), use large pieces of kitchen foil instead. The aim is to seal in all the flavor.

Curried Fish in Banana Leaf

1 fresh whole fish (about 2 lb 4 oz/1 kg in weight), such as salmon or trout, scaled, gutted, and washed

2 teaspoons crushed coriander seeds

2 teaspoons cumin seeds

1 tablespoon grated, fresh coconut (if using dried, see page 85)

½ teaspoon turmeric powder

2 fresh red chiles, deseeded and finely chopped

1 onion, peeled and grated

2 garlic cloves, peeled and crushed

a handful of chopped cilantro leaves

1 tablespoon tamarind water (see page 44) or lemon juice

1 tablespoon vegetable oil

2 or 3 banana leaves

salt

Serves 4–6

Grind the coriander and cumin seeds with a little salt in a pestle and mortar, then pound up with the coconut.

Add the turmeric, chiles, onion, garlic, and cilantro leaves and mix well, then add the tamarind water and the vegetable oil and mix to make a paste.

Make several incisions along the top of the fish and rub in the paste, then rub it inside the cavity of the fish. Marinate in the refrigerator for about 3 hours.

Preheat the oven to 425°F/220°C. Grease the banana leaves and wrap them around the fish. (You can use foil wrapped loosely around the fish if you prefer.)

Bake in the oven for about 30 minutes, then unwrap the leaves or foil and let the fish brown for an additional 7–10 minutes.

All the different flavors in this curry are superb. I'm using Dijon mustard instead of mustard seeds—it's more subtle.

Fish Curry with Mustard

1 lb 4 oz/550 g firm
white fish fillets
(see page 85)

2 tablespoons
poppy seeds

1 tablespoon
Dijon mustard

1 teaspoon
turmeric powder

2 tablespoons
grated fresh coconut
(if using dried,
see page 85)

5–6 garlic
cloves, peeled

½ inch/1 cm piece of
fresh gingerroot,
peeled and grated

3 fresh green chiles

1 onion, peeled
and chopped

2 teaspoons
coriander powder

2 teaspoons
cumin powder

1 teaspoon
chili powder

vegetable oil,
for frying

1 cup fresh
tomato purée

juice of ½ lime

salt

a handful of chopped
cilantro leaves,
to garnish

Serves 4–6

Toast the poppy seeds in a dry skillet gently over low heat for 2 minutes, then take off the heat and soak in water for 10–15 minutes. Pound to a paste in a pestle and mortar.

Put the poppy seeds, mustard, turmeric, coconut, garlic, ginger, fresh green chiles, onion, coriander, cumin and chili powders, and a little salt into a food processor, then whiz to a paste, adding a little water to help the mixture along.

Heat a little vegetable oil in a large pan and cook the paste for 5 minutes, stirring and adding a little more water to make a sauce.

Add the tomato purée and stir-fry for another 5 minutes, then add more water and the lime juice and simmer until you have a rich sauce.

Add the fish fillets and poach them in the sauce until they are cooked. Season, then garnish with the cilantro leaves and serve with plain rice.

Vegetable Curries

This rich, warming, tangy soup makes a delicious appetizer or a substantial entrée. If you are vegetarian, you can substitute vegetable stock for the chicken stock.

Lentil and Mint Soup

1 cup red or yellow lentils, rinsed and drained

unsalted butter and olive oil, for frying

1 large red onion, peeled and finely chopped

2 or 3 garlic cloves, peeled and finely chopped

2 tomatoes, deseeded and finely chopped

2 fresh red chiles, finely chopped

1 heaped tablespoon tomato paste

2 tablespoons paprika

1 oz/25 g long-grain rice

1 tablespoon dried mint

4 cups chicken stock

salt and freshly ground black pepper

For the garnish

2 fresh red chiles, very, very finely chopped

shredded fresh mint leaves

scant 1 stick unsalted butter, melted

Serves 4–6

Heat a little butter and olive oil in a large pan. Stir in the onion and garlic and sauté gently until soft, then stir in the tomatoes and chiles and cook for a couple of minutes.

Add the tomato paste and the paprika. Stir and cook for a couple of minutes, then add the lentils, rice, dried mint, and chicken stock. Simmer gently for 30–40 minutes, or until you have a lovely soup. Taste and season with salt and pepper, and maybe add a little more dried mint. Pour into bowls.

For the garnish, stir the chiles and mint into the melted butter and swirl over each bowl of soup. Serve hot.

There are wonderful flavors and textures to this curry and it is surprisingly rich.

Mixed Dried Fruit Curry

scant ⅔ cup
dried apricots

⅔ cup blanched
almonds

½ cup shelled
pistachios

⅔ cup cashew nuts

1¼ cups plain yogurt

vegetable oil,
for frying

1 cinnamon stick

3 cloves

3 onions, peeled and
finely chopped

½ inch/1 cm piece
of fresh gingerroot,
peeled and chopped

4 garlic cloves, peeled
and finely chopped

4 fresh green chiles,
finely chopped

1 teaspoon
coriander powder

½ teaspoon
cumin powder

1 teaspoon
chili powder

2 tomatoes, chopped

¾ cup walnut pieces

scant ⅔ cup
seedless raisins

¼ teaspoon garam
masala powder

salt

a pinch of
white pepper

4 tablespoons light
cream, to serve

Serves 4–6

Soak the apricots in water for 1½ hours, or until soft, then drain and reserve the water. Soak the almonds and pistachios in hot water for 1 hour. Drain and remove any skins, and reserve the soaking water.

Grind half the cashew nuts, adding a little of the reserved water to make a paste.

Add salt and pepper to the yogurt.

Heat some vegetable oil in a skillet, then add the cinnamon and cloves and cook briefly. Add the onions and cook until golden. Add the ginger, garlic, and fresh chiles and cook for a few minutes.

Add the coriander powder and cook for a couple of minutes, then add the cumin and chili powders and the tomatoes and cook for a couple of minutes.

Take off the heat and remove the cinnamon stick, then whiz the mixture in a food processor to a purée. Pour into a pan, then add the yogurt, cashew paste, and a little of the reserved water. Season to taste and simmer with a lid on for 15 minutes.

In another skillet, cook all the nuts in a little oil, including the remaining cashews, the raisins, and apricots for 5–6 minutes. Add to the sauce and cook for another 10 minutes or so. Add the garam masala powder and cook for a few more minutes, then top with the cream and serve.

This is a wonderful, palate-cleansing, summer dish with bite. It makes
a great appetizer, light but tangy.

Watermelon Curry

½ large watermelon,
skinned, deseeded,
and cut into 1½ inch/
4 cm cubes

2 teaspoons
chili powder

1 teaspoon
turmeric powder

1 teaspoon
coriander powder

2 garlic cloves, peeled
and puréed

vegetable oil,
for frying

½ teaspoon
cumin seeds

2 teaspoons sugar

juice of ½ lime

salt

1 fresh green chile,
deseeded and very
finely chopped,
to garnish

Serves 4–6

Take a handful of the chopped watermelon and whiz in a food processor
to make a juice. Add this juice to the chili, turmeric, and coriander
powders and the garlic purée and add salt to taste.

Heat a little vegetable oil in a pan and add the cumin seeds and cook
for a few seconds, then add the spiced juice.

Reduce the heat and simmer for a few minutes, or until the liquid is
reduced by a third.

Add the sugar and lime juice and cook for another minute, then add the
watermelon cubes and cook on very low heat for 4 minutes, stirring
gently to coat the watermelon in the spices.

Serve sprinkled with the chopped chile.

Asian dishes are very forgiving when it comes to ingredients.
This combination of fruit and vegetables (you can use most of your
favorite vegetables) is delicious and quick.

Mango and Vegetable Curry

approx. 3½ oz/100 g each of the following (or any other vegetable you like), all cut into bite-size pieces: green beans, pumpkin, potato, onion, green bananas

1 large unripe mango, cut into bite-size pieces

2½ dessertspoons turmeric powder

salt

fresh herbs, to garnish

For the masala (curry paste)

8 oz/225 g grated fresh coconut (if using dried, see page 85)

8 small shallots, peeled and chopped

5 fresh green chiles

1 teaspoon cumin seeds

6 fresh curry leaves

Serves 4–6

Put all the ingredients for the masala into a food processor and whiz until you have a paste (add a little water if the mixture is too dry).

Put the vegetable, banana, and mango pieces into a large pan and add enough boiling water to cover. Stir in the turmeric and salt to taste and boil for 5–7 minutes.

When the vegetables are cooked, strain off the cooking liquid and put to one side.

Stir the masala spices into the cooked vegetables and add a small amount of the reserved cooking liquid, then continue to cook until you have a thick spicy gravy.

Serve sprinkled with a handful of fresh herbs.

And why not!

Omelet Curry

3 eggs

1 onion, peeled and
very finely chopped

2 fresh green chiles,
very finely chopped

1 teaspoon chopped
cilantro leaves

vegetable oil,
for frying

salt and freshly
ground black pepper

For the sauce

2 tablespoons
grated fresh coconut
(if using dried,
see page 85)

½ teaspoon
cumin seeds

½ teaspoon
fennel seeds

2 teaspoons
coriander powder

½ teaspoon
chili powder

½ teaspoon
turmeric powder

½ teaspoon garam
masala powder

3 onions, peeled and
finely chopped

3 fresh green chiles,
finely chopped

2 tomatoes,
finely chopped

1 teaspoon
red wine vinegar

a handful of chopped
cilantro leaves

salt

Serves 4–6

To prepare the sauce, put the coconut, cumin and fennel seeds, and coriander, chili, turmeric, and garam masala powders into a food processor, then whiz together with a little water to make a paste. Set aside.

To make the omelet, whisk the eggs, then add the onion, green chiles, and cilantro leaves and season to taste. Heat a little oil in a skillet and pour in the omelet mixture. When the underneath is cooked, flip the omelet over and cook the other side until it is golden and well set. Remove from the heat and cut into strips, then roll up the strips and set aside.

To finish the sauce, heat some oil in a skillet and cook the onions until they are soft and starting to brown. Add the spice paste and stir-fry for about 5 minutes.

Add the green chiles and tomatoes and sauté for 5 minutes, then add the vinegar, about generous 2 cups of water, and season to taste. Simmer for 10 minutes, then add the omelet strips and chopped cilantro. Heat through for 3–4 minutes, then serve.

Paneer is an Indian form of cottage cheese, but quite unlike cottage cheese as we know it. It is firm in texture, looking a little like tofu. It absorbs flavors well. Do try to get (or make) the real thing for this recipe. Nothing else will really do.

Paneer and Vegetable Curry

ghee or clarified butter, for frying

1 lb/450 g paneer (Indian cheese), cut into approx. 1 inch/2.5 cm cubes

1 red onion, peeled and finely sliced

1 teaspoon cumin powder

1 teaspoon ground ginger

½ teaspoon chili powder

1 lb/450 g frozen peas

2 or 3 tomatoes, finely chopped

salt

Serves 4–6

Melt some ghee in a skillet, then add the paneer and cook until golden brown. Take out of the pan and set aside on paper towels to drain.

Add the onion to the pan and cook until soft and slightly colored.

Add the spices and salt and cook for a couple more minutes to release the flavors, then add the peas and tomatoes and stir well until the vegetables are coated with the spicy mixture.

Add the paneer and stir well until all the ingredients are combined and the paneer is heated through. Serve.

Paneer goes well with spinach in this simple curry. Serve as a side dish or with some bread as a course in its own right.

Paneer with Spinach

14 oz/400 g paneer (Indian cheese; see page 107), cut into cubes

1 lb 12 oz/800 g spinach, washed and well drained

ghee or clarified butter, for frying

1 teaspoon cumin seeds

3 garlic cloves, peeled and finely chopped

2 teaspoons coriander powder

1 teaspoon chili powder

salt

scant ½ cup heavy cream, to serve

Serves 4–6

Heat a little ghee in a skillet and cook the cheese until golden brown on all sides. Set aside.

Stir-fry the spinach in a little ghee until well softened, then whiz to a purée in a food processor.

Heat some more ghee and add the cumin seeds and garlic and sauté until golden brown.

Add the coriander and chili powders and the spinach, then season and stir-fry for a couple of minutes. Add the paneer and simmer gently for about 5 minutes.

Put the mixture into a dish, then top with the cream and serve.

Do take the trouble to find the right mushrooms for this dish. White mushrooms do not have the necessary flavor. It may look like a complicated recipe, but it is really worth the trouble for that authentic Chinese taste.

Chili Mushrooms with Cashew Nuts

12 oz/350 g oyster or Chinese mushrooms, chopped into bite-size pieces

1 inch/2.5 cm piece of fresh gingerroot, peeled and grated

vegetable oil, for frying

4 garlic cloves, peeled and finely sliced

½ inch/1 cm piece of fresh gingerroot, peeled and finely sliced

2 dried chiles, crumbled

2 scallions, cut into 1 inch/ 2.5 cm lengths

2 teaspoons cornstarch

For the garnish

1 teaspoon sesame seeds

2 tablespoons cashew nuts, fried gently for about 1 minute

For the sauce

½ cup chicken or strong vegetable stock

2 tablespoons chili sauce

1 tablespoon Chinese black vinegar or balsamic vinegar

1 tablespoon dark soy sauce

2 teaspoons oyster sauce

1 teaspoon sesame oil

½ teaspoon Chinese five-spice powder

1 teaspoon sugar

Serves 4–6

Put the grated ginger in a small pan, then cover with water and boil for about 1 minute. Strain and keep the water, discarding the ginger.

Blanch the mushrooms in the ginger water for about 1 minute, then drain well. Cook the mushrooms in hot vegetable oil for about 1 minute to seal, then drain and set aside.

Put all the sauce ingredients into a small bowl, then mix together and set aside.

Heat some more oil in a wok or heavy-bottomed pan and stir-fry the garlic, sliced ginger, and chiles for about 30 seconds.

Add the mushrooms and scallions and stir-fry for about 1 minute, then add the sauce to the pan and cook for 1 minute.

Add the cornstarch and cook for about 30 seconds to thicken the mixture.

Put on a serving dish and garnish with the sesame seeds and cashew nuts.

Almost everyone has eggs in their refrigerator and this is a great way of using them for the curry lover.

The tanginess and texture of green tomatoes is essential for this dish, and for those of you who grow your own tomatoes, this is a great way of using those that refuse to ripen. It can be eaten like a chutney, as an accompaniment, but also stands on its own as a main dish.

Curried Eggs

Curried Green Tomatoes

4 hard-cooked eggs, shelled and cut in half

chopped cilantro leaves, to garnish

For the masala (curry paste)

2 or 3 garlic cloves, peeled and crushed

1 inch/2.5 cm piece of fresh gingerroot, finely grated

1 teaspoon each of turmeric, cumin, fennel, and chili powders

1 tablespoon coriander powder

For the sauce

vegetable oil, for frying

1 teaspoon fenugreek seeds

1 teaspoon fennel seeds

1 small cinnamon stick

1 large onion, peeled and finely chopped

2 or 3 tomatoes, finely chopped

14 fl oz/400 ml canned coconut milk

salt and freshly ground black pepper

Put all the ingredients for the masala with a little water into a food processor and whiz to a paste, then put to one side.

For the sauce, heat a little vegetable oil in a pan. Add the fenugreek and fennel seeds and the cinnamon stick and stir-fry for a couple of seconds. Add the onion and cook until soft, then stir in the tomatoes. Add the curry paste and stir-fry for a minute, then stir in the coconut milk and simmer until you have a smooth, rich gravy. If this appears to be too thick, thin with a little water. Season to taste.

Put the hard-cooked eggs gently into the gravy and heat to warm through. Serve garnished with the chopped cialntro.

Serves 4–6

1 lb 2 oz/500 g unripe green tomatoes, chopped

1 teaspoon chili powder

2 teaspoons coriander powder

1 teaspoon turmeric powder

2 garlic cloves, peeled and puréed

1 teaspoon sugar

vegetable oil, for frying

½ teaspoon cumin seeds

½ teaspoon fenugreek seeds

3 fresh green chiles, finely chopped

salt

Put the chili, coriander, and turmeric powders, the garlic, and sugar into a small bowl. Mix together and add a little water to form a paste.

Heat some vegetable oil in a large pan and cook the cumin and fenugreek seeds for a few seconds, then add the paste and cook for a couple of minutes.

Add the tomatoes and fresh chiles, then season with salt and cook, stirring occasionally, until the tomatoes are softened.

Serves 4–6

This is a little bit of a variation on stuffed bell peppers. Do not overcook this dish, as the tomatoes will collapse and lose some of their flavor. You can leave out the peanuts if you wish.

Hot Stuffed Tomatoes

4 large ripe tomatoes

14 oz/400 g canned cooked lentils, rinsed and drained

5 oz/150 g paneer (Indian cheese, see page 107), grated

vegetable oil, for frying

1 tablespoon cumin seeds

½ inch/1 cm piece of fresh gingerroot, peeled and grated

1 teaspoon chili powder

1 fresh green chile, very finely chopped

1 dessertspoon chopped unsalted peanuts

1 teaspoon sugar

a handful of chopped cilantro leaves, plus extra to garnish

salt

Serves 4–6

Preheat the oven to 400°F/200°C. Put the lentils into a food processor and whiz enough to break them down. Then put them into a bowl and mix with the paneer.

Cut the tops off the tomatoes and scoop out and reserve the flesh.

Heat a little vegetable oil in a heavy-bottomed pan and add the cumin seeds, ginger, chili powder, fresh chile, peanuts, sugar, chopped cilantro, and salt. Cook for about 1 minute, then add the tomato flesh and cook for another minute.

Add the lentils and paneer and mix well together for another couple of minutes.

Stuff the tomatoes with the lentil mixture and cook in the oven for about 10 minutes.

Serve hot, garnished with the chopped cilantro leaves.

Although the sauce is a little fiddly, this is a delicious vegetable dish and worth the trouble.

Vegetable Brochettes with Tofu and Cinnamon

1 zucchini, cut into slices of medium thickness

1 large onion, peeled and cut into wedges

1 red bell pepper, cut into 1 inch/2.5 cm squares

vegetable oil, for frying

8–10 white mushrooms

1–2 cakes firm tofu, cut into 1 inch/ 2.5 cm square chunks

For the sauce

2 garlic cloves, peeled and finely chopped

4 shallots, peeled and finely chopped

1 inch/2.5 cm piece of fresh gingerroot, peeled and grated

1 fresh red chile, finely chopped

1 fresh green chile, finely chopped

½ cup chicken stock

2 tablespoons Thai sweet soy sauce

2 tablespoons coriander seeds, toasted and crushed

½ teaspoon coriander powder

½ teaspoon cinnamon powder

½ teaspoon freshly grated nutmeg

½ teaspoon white pepper

a pinch of ground cloves

salt

Serves 4–6

Blanch the zucchini slices, onion wedges, and bell pepper squares in boiling water for 2 minutes, then remove and drain.

Heat a little vegetable oil in a pan and cook the tofu on all sides until it is golden brown.

To make the sauce, heat some oil in a small pan and stir-fry the garlic, shallots, ginger, and chiles until they have softened.

Add all the other sauce ingredients and bring to a boil, then reduce the heat and simmer until the sauce reduces by about half. Cool, then whiz in a food processor until smooth.

Thread alternate pieces of zucchini, red bell pepper, onion, mushroom, and tofu onto skewers and brush with the sauce.

Cook on a grill, under a hot broiler, or on a grill pan, turning the skewers until the vegetables have cooked.

This is a wonderfully colorful, spicy and filling dish, whether you are vegetarian or not!

Red or Green Bell Peppers Stuffed with Spicy Lentils

4 red or green bell peppers with their tops cut off (retain the tops), deseeded and pith removed

400 g/14 oz canned cooked lentils, rinsed and drained

ghee, butter, or vegetable oil, for frying

2 red onions, peeled and finely diced

2 or 3 fresh green chiles, finely chopped

1 inch/2.5 cm piece of fresh gingerroot, peeled and finely grated

1 teaspoon cumin seeds

3 teaspoons freshly ground coriander seeds

salt and freshly ground black pepper

chopped cilantro leaves, to garnish

Serves 4–6

Heat some ghee in a pan and gently cook the onions, chiles, and ginger until they are soft.

Stir in the spices and season with salt and pepper, then cook for about 5 minutes, or until all the ingredients are well amalgamated. Remove from the heat and mix in the lentils.

Preheat the oven to 375°F/190°C. Stuff the bell peppers with the lentil and spice mixture, then replace the lids of the bell peppers and paint them generously with ghee. Put the bell peppers in a baking dish and cover lightly with tin foil. Bake in the oven for about 30 minutes, basting from time to time with more ghee.

Serve garnished with chopped cilantro.

These barely need an introduction—we all order them when we are at the local Indian restaurant. But they are so simple to make, and they are so much more delicious than anything you can buy.

A lovely, creamy dish that can be eaten either as an appetizer or as a vegetable accompaniment to a main dish.

Onion Bhajis

Spiced Pearl Onions in Yogurt

2 onions, peeled and finely sliced

⅔ cup besan, sifted to remove any lumps

1 teaspoon coriander powder

1 teaspoon cumin powder

2 fresh green chiles, deseeded and finely chopped

vegetable oil, for deep-frying

salt

Serves 4–6

Put the besan, coriander and cumin powders, the chiles, a little vegetable oil, and warm water and salt to taste into a food processor and whiz until you have a smooth batter.

Put the batter aside for about 30 minutes, then stir in the onion slices.

Heat the vegetable oil in a deep-fat fryer, then gently drop spoonfuls of the batter mixture into the pan—about 3 at a time. When they are golden, lift out and drain on paper towels. Serve hot as an appetizer or as an entrée with salad.

1 lb 2 oz/500 g pearl onions, peeled and cut into fourths

1 teaspoon chili powder

2 teaspoons coriander powder

2 teaspoons turmeric powder

¼ cup plain yogurt

vegetable oil, for frying

1 teaspoon cumin seeds

2 garlic cloves, peeled and crushed

1 inch/2.5 cm piece of fresh gingerroot, peeled and grated

salt

Serves 4–6

Mix together the chili, coriander, and turmeric powders and the yogurt with a little water and put to one side.

Heat some oil in a pan and cook the cumin seeds for a few seconds, then stir in the garlic and ginger and stir-fry for a few seconds.

Add the yogurt mixture and the onions, stirring to coat them well.

Add about 1½ cups of water and simmer over low heat until the onions are tender. Add salt to taste.

Even the most common, simple vegetables make wonderful curries. They are healthy since they are generally cooked very quickly, thus retaining the nutrients. As with all curries, you can make them hotter or milder as you prefer.

Okra, or ladies' fingers, are a delicious vegetable, now widely available. They are wonderful in curries, but be aware when you cook them that they initially appear to go rather sticky—don't panic! As they cook, the stickiness goes.

Carrots and Cauliflower with Chile and Ginger

Spiced Okra

6 or 7 carrots, sliced into rounds, or baby carrots left whole

7 oz/200 g cauliflower florets

vegetable oil, for frying

3 shallots, peeled and finely sliced

1 or 2 garlic cloves, peeled and finely sliced

4 scallions, sliced into 1 inch/ 2.5 cm lengths

1 tablespoon light soy sauce

a dash of fish sauce

1 fresh red chile, finely chopped

a pinch of ground ginger

Serves 4–6

Blanch the carrots and cauliflower in boiling water for about 3 minutes, then drain and set aside.

Heat some vegetable oil in a wok or skillet and cook the shallots for a minute or two until soft, then add the garlic and cook for an additional minute, taking care not to burn the garlic.

Add the scallions, soy and fish sauces, carrots, and cauliflower and stir-fry for a couple of minutes.

Finally, add the chile and ginger and stir-fry for 2 minutes more. Serve hot.

14 oz/400 g okra, washed and cut into chunks

vegetable oil, for frying

½ teaspoon garam masala powder

1 inch/2.5 cm piece of fresh gingerroot, peeled and grated

1 teaspoon turmeric powder

1 fresh green chile, finely chopped

1¼ cups plain yogurt

a good handful of cilantro, coarsely chopped

salt

Serves 4–6

Heat a little vegetable oil in a pan. Add the garam masala powder and stir-fry for a few seconds until the aroma is released, then add the okra. Cook for about 5 minutes, stirring, then add the ginger, turmeric, chile, and salt to taste. Stir-fry for about another minute.

Add a little water to moisten, then cook gently, stirring occasionally, until the okra is cooked.

Stir in the yogurt and heat through.

At the last minute, stir in the cilantro and serve hot.

Homemade dal makes a wonderful side dish to most curries. Eaten with naan bread or roti (see pages 133, 135), it makes a spicy, creamy appetizer dish.

Cauliflower is not the most flavorsome vegetable around, but soaks up other flavors very well. This makes either a substantial side dish or an entrée.

Spicy Dal

Cauliflower Dal

1 cup green lentils, rinsed and drained

1 teaspoon turmeric powder

vegetable oil, for frying

1 teaspoon cumin seeds

2 red onions, peeled and finely chopped

1 inch/2.5 cm piece of fresh gingerroot, peeled and grated

2 garlic cloves, peeled and crushed

1 dessertspoon chili powder

3 tomatoes, finely chopped

salt

Serves 4–6

Put the lentils in a pan, then cover with water and add the turmeric and salt to taste. Cook until tender.

Heat a little vegetable oil in a pan and add the cumin seeds. Cook for a couple of minutes, then add the onions and stir-fry until brown. Stir in the ginger, garlic, and chili powder, then add the tomatoes.

Cook this sauce for about 20 minutes until puréed, then add the lentils and simmer for 5–7 minutes.

1 lb 2 oz/500 g cauliflower florets

vegetable oil, for frying

2 red onions, peeled and finely chopped

2 garlic cloves, peeled and finely chopped

1 inch/2.5 cm piece of fresh gingerroot, peeled and grated

4 fresh red chiles, finely chopped

1 teaspoon coriander powder

1 teaspoon cumin powder

½ teaspoon garam masala powder

scant ⅓ cup small green lentils, rinsed and drained

1¼ cups vegetable stock

14 fl oz/400 ml canned coconut milk

generous 1 cup peas

a good handful of cilantro leaves, chopped

juice of ½ lemon

salt

Serves 4–6

Heat a little vegetable oil in a pan and gently cook the onions, garlic, ginger, chiles, and spices until the onions have softened.

Add the lentils and stock and simmer for about 10 minutes.

Add the cauliflower and coconut milk to the lentils, then simmer for another 10 minutes.

Stir in the peas, chopped cilantro, and lemon juice, then bring to a simmer and cook for a couple of minutes or until the peas are cooked. Season with salt and serve.

For this recipe from Singapore, you must use firm tofu. It has little flavor itself, but soaks up other flavors like a sponge. The rich peanut sauce is perfect in this dish.

Chilied Tofu Salad with Peanut Sauce

400 g/14 oz firm tofu, drained and cut into 1 inch/2.5 cm cubes

vegetable oil, for frying

1 dried red chile

2 oz/50 g cucumber, deseeded and cut into 1½ inch/4 cm strips

2 oz/50 g carrot, peeled and cut into 1½ inch/4 cm strips

generous ⅓ cup fine green beans, trimmed and blanched for 1 minute

2 scallions, cut into 1½ inch/4 cm strips

mixed salad greens

1 fresh red chile, deseeded and cut into very fine strips

1 tablespoon coarsely chopped peanuts, to garnish

For the peanut sauce

⅔ cup unsalted peanuts

4 garlic cloves, peeled

1 large fresh red chile

1½ tablespoons soft brown sugar

4 teaspoons white wine vinegar

3 tablespoons dark soy sauce

Serves 4–6

Put all the ingredients for the peanut sauce with ½ cup of water into a food processor and whiz until you have a thick, smooth sauce. Set aside.

Heat some vegetable oil in a heavy-bottomed pan, then add the dried red chile and stir to release its flavor into the oil.

Add the tofu cubes to the oil and cook for about 4 minutes, turning them regularly, until they are golden brown. Drain on paper towels and discard the dried chile.

Mix the tofu with all the salad ingredients and the fresh chile and add to the bowl of peanut sauce. Toss the mixture together, then transfer to a serving dish. Sprinkle over the chopped peanuts and serve.

Particularly in Malaysia, salads are very popular and they can be warm, as this one is, or cold. The addition of nuts makes for a crunchy texture, but you can leave them out if you prefer.

Hot Salad with Peanut Sauce

1 potato, peeled and finely sliced

vegetable oil for frying

3½ oz/100 g each of:
shredded cabbage;
cauliflower florets;
string beans, sliced;
baby carrots, sliced;
bean sprouts

For the peanut sauce

vegetable oil for frying

⅔ cup unsalted peanuts

1 garlic clove, peeled and very finely chopped

2 shallots, peeled and very finely chopped

a dash of fish sauce

1 small fresh green chile, very finely chopped

1 teaspoon brown sugar

1 cup coconut cream

lemon juice

salt

For the garnish

½ cucumber, peeled and finely sliced

2 tablespoons chopped peanuts

1 onion, peeled, finely sliced, and fried until crispy

Serves 4–6

To make the sauce, heat some vegetable oil in a skillet or wok and cook the peanuts for 5 minutes, stirring all the time. Drain the peanuts on paper towels, then whiz to a powder in a food processor.

Using a pestle and mortar, pound the garlic, shallots, fish sauce, and chile to a fine paste, using a little salt to help the process. Cook this paste in a little oil for 1 minute, stirring all the time, then add the sugar and 1¾ cups of water and bring to a boil.

Add the peanut powder and simmer until the mixture has thickened, then add the coconut cream, stirring well until all the ingredients are well mixed. Set aside, keeping the sauce warm.

To make the salad, cook the potato slices in a little vegetable oil until crisp and brown. Blanch the other vegetables in boiling water for 4–5 minutes, then drain and set aside.

Arrange the cucumber slices on one side of a serving dish and the potatoes on the other side. Put the blanched vegetables in the center of the dish.

Add the lemon juice to the peanut sauce and pour it over the vegetables. Garnish with the chopped peanuts and fried onion.

This is a really refreshing salad with a bit of a kick in the tail. It can be served on its own or with fishcakes or rissoles.

A lovely crunchy salad with a spicy dressing, this would be good in winter—and it's good for you!

Thai Salad

Vegetable Salad

½ firm white cabbage, shredded

2 carrots, peeled and grated

2 scallions, cut into very fine strips

1 fresh red chile, deseeded and cut into very fine strips

1 tablespoon ground dried shrimp (optional)

For the dressing

1 tablespoon fish sauce

2 teaspoons sugar

2 garlic cloves, peeled and crushed

2 tablespoons lime juice

freshly ground black pepper

Serves 4–6

Mix all the salad ingredients together in a large bowl.

Mix all the dressing ingredients together thoroughly in a bowl.

Pour the dressing onto the salad and toss together, then serve.

½ firm white cabbage, finely shredded

5 carrots, peeled and grated

3 red onions, peeled and thinly sliced

3½ oz/100 g string beans, thinly sliced

salt

a handful of crushed, unsalted peanuts, to garnish

For the dressing

2 small fresh red chiles, finely chopped

1 inch/2.5 cm piece of fresh gingerroot, peeled and finely chopped

3 garlic cloves, peeled and finely chopped

½ cup groundnut oil

scant ¼ cup white wine vinegar

1 teaspoon curry powder

1 teaspoon mustard seeds, crushed

½ teaspoon turmeric powder

Serves 4–6

Mix together all the vegetables in a large bowl.

Mix together all the ingredients for the dressing and toss the vegetables in the dressing.

Season with salt and sprinkle on the peanuts, then serve.

This is a summery salad dressed with Asian flavors of sesame, coriander, lime, and ginger.

Not one for the faint-hearted among you. This is full of flavor, with lots of chile.

Spicy Salad

Floyd's Salad

1 crisp lettuce, chopped

½ cucumber, peeled, deseeded and chopped into cubes

1 red onion, peeled and finely sliced

1 red bell pepper, deseeded and chopped into ½ inch/1 cm chunks

1 green bell pepper, deseeded and chopped into ½ inch/1 cm chunks

5 tomatoes, skinned, deseeded, and chopped

For the dressing

4 fresh green chiles, finely chopped

1 tablespoon sesame oil

½ teaspoon coriander powder

½ teaspoon chili powder

½ teaspoon ground ginger

juice of ½ lime

salt and freshly ground black pepper

Serves 4–6

Mix together the lettuce, cucumber, onion, bell peppers, and tomatoes in a large bowl and season with salt.

In a small bowl, mix together all the dressing ingredients and season with salt and pepper.

Pour the dressing over the salad and toss well to coat.

3 red onions, peeled and very finely sliced

1 large fresh green chile, deseeded and very finely sliced into strips

1 large fresh red chile, deseeded and very finely sliced into strips

1 inch/2.5 cm piece of fresh gingerroot, peeled and very finely sliced into strips

1 large bunch of flatleaf parsley, stems removed

1 large bunch of cilantro leaves, stems removed

walnut oil

Serves 4–6

Put all the ingredients except the walnut oil in a bowl and mix. Sprinkle over the walnut oil and mix well, then serve as an accompaniment.

Rice, Breads, and Chutneys

This makes a change from plain rice as an accompaniment. It is a bit more substantial.

Dill is a very aromatic herb that accompanies fish dishes so well, so this rice dish is wonderful with fish or seafood kabobs.

Savory Lentils and Rice

Rice with Dill

generous ¾ cup green lentils

1¾ cups long-grain rice, washed under cold running water until the water runs clear

scant ½ cup ghee or clarified butter

1 onion, peeled and finely chopped

2 garlic cloves, peeled and finely chopped

8 cloves

4 cardamom pods, crushed

1 cinnamon stick

1½ teaspoons turmeric powder

salt and freshly ground black pepper

Serves 8–10

Put the lentils and rice into a large bowl and soak in cold water for 2 hours.

Heat the ghee butter in a skillet and gently cook the onion and garlic until they are soft.

Add the spices and seasonings and stir-fry for 3–4 minutes.

Drain the rice and lentils and add to the onion, garlic, and spices in the skillet, stirring well to make sure all the grains are coated in the mixture.

Add 3½ cups of boiling water and bring to a boil, then cover and simmer for 20–30 minutes, or until the grains are tender.

Remove the lid and leave on the heat, stirring constantly, until all the liquid has been absorbed. Serve immediately.

1 cup long-grain rice, washed under cold running water until the water runs clear

vegetable oil, for frying

2 green cardamom pods, crushed

1 fresh green chile, very finely chopped

a good handful of fresh dill, finely chopped

salt

Serves 4–6

Heat a little vegetable oil in a pan, then add the cardamom pods and chile and stir-fry for about 1 minute.

Add the dill and salt to taste and sauté for 1 minute.

Add 1½ cups of water and bring to a boil, then add the rice and cook until all the liquid has been absorbed and the rice is tender.

Serve with your favorite fish dish.

Rice is all too often served plain, accompanying another dish;
however, it absorbs other flavors so well. This dish would stand
proudly on its own, with the addition of cashew nuts giving it texture.

Spicy Lemon Rice

1½ cups long-grain rice, washed under cold running water until the water runs clear

ghee or clarified butter

vegetable oil, for frying

1 teaspoon black mustard seeds

10 fresh curry leaves

1 fresh green chile, finely chopped

4 dried red chiles, crushed

1 inch/2.5 cm piece of fresh gingerroot, peeled and grated

a handful of unsalted cashew nuts

½ teaspoon turmeric powder

juice of 2 lemons

a good handful of cilantro leaves, chopped, to garnish

Serves 6

Boil the rice in a very large pan with plenty of salted water until tender, then drain well. Preheat the oven to 300°F/150°C.

Drop a dollop of ghee into the rice and stir well. Transfer the rice to an ovenproof dish, then cover with foil and keep warm in the oven.

Heat some vegetable oil in a pan, then add the mustard seeds and stir them around until they crackle. Add the curry leaves, fresh and dried chiles, the ginger, and cashew nuts and stir-fry for about 30 seconds.

Stir in the turmeric powder, lemon juice, and a dash of water to moisten and cook for 3 minutes, or until you have a yellow gravy. Stir this into the rice until all the ingredients are combined and garnish with the chopped cilantro.

An aromatic rice that goes particularly well with lamb dishes.

Spicy and slightly caramelized, this rice dish is a great accompaniment to most meat dishes.

Saffron Rice with Cumin

Browned Rice

1½ cups long-grain rice, washed under cold running water until the water runs clear

2 teaspoons cumin seeds

a pinch of saffron strands

salt

Serves 4–6

Toast the cumin seeds in a dry skillet for a few seconds until they release their aroma.

Boil the rice with the saffron in plenty of salted water.

When the rice is cooked, drain and stir in the toasted cumin seeds.

1 lb 4 oz/550 g basmati rice, soaked for 15 minutes

vegetable oil, for frying

2 onions, peeled and finely sliced

1 cinnamon stick

1 bay leaf

5 cloves

1 teaspoon freshly grated nutmeg

2 teaspoons sugar

salt

Serves 8–10

Wash the soaked rice under lots of cold running water until the water runs clear and drain.

Heat a little vegetable oil in a pan and cook the onions until they are well browned.

Add the cinnamon, bay leaf, cloves, and nutmeg and sauté for 5 minutes.

Add the sugar and let it caramelize, but do not let it burn.

Add the rice and sauté for a couple of minutes, then season to taste and add plenty of boiling water. Cover the pan and cook over medium heat for 9–10 minutes, or until the rice is tender and the water has been absorbed.

This is quite a hot rice dish, and the coconut adds a great texture to the finished item. Coconut rice is good with grilled fish or meat.

This is not the fried rice we know and love from the local restaurant. The flavors really come through!

Coconut Rice

1¼ cups basmati rice, soaked for 15 minutes

150 g/5 oz grated fresh coconut (if using dried, see page 85)

vegetable oil, for frying

1 teaspoon mustard seeds

5 dried red chiles, crushed

3 fresh green chiles, deseeded and finely chopped

2 garlic cloves, peeled and finely chopped

4 cardamom pods, crushed

1 inch/2.5 cm piece of fresh gingerroot, peeled and grated

1 teaspoon turmeric powder

10 fresh curry leaves

ghee or clarified butter

salt

a good handful of chopped cilantro leaves, to garnish

Wash the soaked rice under lots of cold running water until the water runs clear and drain.

Boil the rice in plenty of salted water for about 7 minutes, then drain and place in a dish to dry out.

Toast the coconut in a dry skillet until golden brown.

Heat some vegetable oil in a pan. Add the mustard seeds and stir-fry for about 30 seconds, then add the dried and fresh chiles, the garlic, cardamom pods, and ginger and stir-fry for another 30 seconds.

Add the turmeric and curry leaves and stir-fry for 30 seconds, then add the coconut and rice and stir-fry for 2 minutes.

Remove from the heat and cover for 1 hour to let the flavors infuse, then stir in the ghee.

Reheat either in the oven or on the stove, stirring occasionally, and garnish with the chopped cilantro.

Serves 4–6

Fried Rice

scant 1 cup basmati rice, washed under cold running water until the water runs clear, then soaked for 30 minutes

vegetable oil, for frying

2 small red onions, peeled and finely chopped

8 cloves

4 cardamom pods, crushed

1 teaspoon cumin seeds

1 teaspoon coriander seeds

1 cinnamon stick

1 bay leaf

salt

Drain the rice and reserve the soaking water. Put both to one side.

Heat some vegetable oil in a skillet and stir-fry the onions until they are just soft, then add all the remaining ingredients and continue sautéeing to release the flavor of the spices.

Add the rice to the pan and stir-fry for about 2 minutes, or until the rice is well coated with the flavorings.

Tip in enough of the soaking water to cover the rice and simmer for about 12 minutes, or until the water is absorbed and the rice is cooked.

Serves 3–4

This recipe is very simple, if a little time-consuming, but worth it for that authentic Indian taste.

Simple Naan Bread

1⅔ cups white bread flour

1 teaspoon salt

1 teaspoon active dry yeast

1 teaspoon honey

¼ stick butter, melted

Sift the flour and salt into a large bowl and sprinkle in the yeast. Make a well in the center and add ¾ cup of warm water, the honey, and butter and mix together well.

Knead until you have a silky dough, then cover and let stand in a warm place for 1 hour, or until the dough has doubled in size.

Knead again to knock out the air and shape as required—either several small breads or one big one. Cover and set aside to rise for 15 minutes. Preheat the oven to 450°F/230°C and put a baking sheet in to heat up.

Put the risen dough on the hot baking sheet and bake for 10 minutes, or until golden brown.

In India, bread is a very popular accompaniment to curry. It is used for scooping up the lovely sauces and chutneys. Flavored with spinach, this bread makes a colorful and simple snack.

This flat bread is served all the time in India, for breakfast, lunch, and dinner and for snacks throughout the day.

Spinach Bread

1 teaspoon cumin seeds

2½ oz/60 g cooked spinach with all the liquid squeezed out

1½ cups whole-wheat flour

salt

ghee or clarified butter, to serve

Toast the cumin seeds in a dry skillet for a few seconds, then grind them lightly with the back of a spoon to break them up.

Mix together the cumin, spinach, flour, and salt to taste and add water a little at a time to make a dough. Divide the dough into 6 separate balls and roll each flat with a rolling pin into a disk.

Toast the disks on each side in a dry skillet until they are browned. Paint each with a little ghee and serve.

Roti

scant ¾ cup whole-wheat flour

1 teaspoon ghee or vegetable oil

Mix the flour with generous ¼ cup of warm water.

Add the ghee and knead thoroughly for at least 7 minutes, or until the texture is smooth and soft. Cover and let stand for 1 hour.

Shape the dough and cook in a hot dry skillet for about 2 minutes on each side, or until lightly browned.

Chutneys and salsas are so easy to make and add so much to a dish. Most chutneys will keep comfortably in the refrigerator for at least a week, salsas probably just for a couple of days.

Fresh Mango Chutney

2 slightly underripe mangoes, peeled and thinly sliced

a handful of chopped cashew nuts

1 fresh red chile, finely chopped

a handful of raisins

a handful of chopped fresh mint leaves

½ teaspoon cumin powder

½ teaspoon coriander powder

1 teaspoon soft brown sugar

½ teaspoon turmeric powder

Put the mango slices into a bowl, then add the rest of the ingredients and stir gently until they are thoroughly mixed. Chill in the refrigerator for at least 2 hours.

Serve with naan bread, pappadams, or your favorite curry.

Sweet Mango Chutney

2 large unripe mangoes, peeled and cut into small cubes

1 lb 2 oz/500 g pure cane sugar

1 tablespoon chili powder

½ tablespoon fennel seeds

1 teaspoon fenugreek seeds

1 tablespoon white wine vinegar

a good pinch of salt

1 teaspoon small black mustard seeds

oil, for preserving

Preheat the oven to 350°F/180°C. Mix together all the ingredients except the mustard seeds and oil.

Put the mixture in a tight-lidded jar and cook in a bain-marie in the oven for about 1 hour, or until the ingredients have softened (you could also do this on top of the stove).

When the jar has cooled down, sprinkle the mustard seeds on top and cover the chutney with oil.

Seal and refrigerate for 2–3 weeks before using.

Cucumber Chutney

Sweet and Sour Chutney

1 cucumber, peeled, deseeded, and cut into batons

¼ cup white wine vinegar

1 inch/2.5 cm piece of fresh gingerroot, peeled and very finely diced

5 small fresh green chiles, very finely chopped

salt

Put the vinegar, salt, and a dash of water into a pan and bring to a boil. While still boiling, add the ginger and cucumber and cook for a couple of minutes, or until the cucumber is just softening.

Bring off the heat, then pop into a clean jar or bowl and stir in the green chiles. Refrigerate overnight before using.

6 tablespoons grated fresh coconut (if using dried, see page 85)

a large bunch of cilantro leaves

1 inch/2.5 cm piece of fresh gingerroot, peeled and finely chopped

6 fresh green chiles

4 garlic cloves, peeled

1 teaspoon coriander seeds

a dash of white wine vinegar

sugar

salt

Place all the ingredients except the sugar and salt into a food processor and whiz to a smooth paste. Add sugar and salt to taste.

Beet Raita

6 cooked baby beets
(not in vinegar),
peeled

1¼ cups plain yogurt

1 teaspoon sugar

a handful of finely
chopped chives, plus
extra to garnish

a pinch of cayenne
pepper

salt

Cut the beet into thin slices and arrange
in a serving dish.

Mix together the yogurt, sugar, chives,
cayenne pepper, and salt and chill in
the refrigerator for 30 minutes.

Pour the yogurt mixture over the beet
slices and garnish with more chopped
chives.

Cilantro and Mint Chutney

a large handful of
cilantro leaves

a large handful of
fresh mint leaves

2 apples, peeled,
cored, and cut
into cubes

Whiz all the ingredients together in
a food processor until you have a
wonderfully aromatic paste.

Spicy Lime Pickle

10–12 limes,
cut into wedges

3 teaspoons
fenugreek seeds

3 teaspoons
mustard seeds

5 teaspoons
chili powder

1 fresh green chile,
finely chopped

3 teaspoons
turmeric powder

1 cup–scant 1¼ cups
vegetable oil

salt

Put the lime wedges into a bowl, then
sprinkle with salt and let stand for
10–15 minutes.

Roast the fenugreek and mustard seeds
in a dry skillet for a minute or so to
release their aromas, then grind to a
powder in a pestle and mortar.

Add the chili powder, fresh chile, and
turmeric powder and mix well, then
sprinkle this mixture over the limes and
stir all the ingredients together.

Add the vegetable oil, then cover the
bowl with a dry cloth and let stand in
a warm place for about a week. Then
put the pickle into jars and store in
the refrigerator for about 2 weeks
before using.

Coconut Chutney

4 tablespoons
white lentils, rinsed
and drained

8 oz/225 g grated
fresh coconut (or, if
you are using dried
coconut, soak it for
1 hour in a little
coconut milk)

6 fresh green chiles

2 fresh red chiles

1 inch/2.5 cm piece
of fresh gingerroot,
peeled

1 teaspoon black
mustard seeds

a little coconut milk

10–12 fresh
curry leaves

Gently roast the white lentils in a dry skillet, being careful not to burn them.

Put the lentils with all the other ingredients except the curry leaves into a food processor and blend thoroughly, softening with enough coconut milk to make a paste.

Tip into a bowl and mix in the curry leaves. Refrigerate until needed.

Tomato Chutney

400 g/14 oz cherry
tomatoes, cut
into fourths

4–6 scallions,
chopped

1 fresh green chile,
finely chopped

a handful of cilantro
leaves, chopped

a dash of lemon juice

a pinch of
cayenne pepper

salt

Mix the tomatoes with the scallions, chile, cilantro leaves, and salt to taste.

Stir gently together, then add a squeeze of lemon juice and the cayenne pepper. Mix once more, then cover and place in the refrigerator for at least 1 hour before using.

Raita

chopped mint

diced tomato

diced cucumber

chopped fresh chiles

chopped scallions

plain yogurt

Mix any or all of the ingredients with enough plain yogurt to make a dropping consistency.

5 inch/12.5 cm chunk of cucumber, peeled, deseeded, and finely chopped

2 large tomatoes, skinned, deseeded, and finely chopped

2 fresh green chiles, finely chopped

1 red onion, peeled and finely chopped

½ teaspoon chili powder

a handful of cilantro leaves, finely chopped

juice of 2 or 3 limes

salt

Mix all the ingredients together in a large bowl and place in the refrigerator for about 30 minutes. Use on the same day.

Sweet Chili Sauce

10 fresh green chiles, deseeded and chopped

4 garlic cloves, peeled

1 tablespoon fish sauce

juice of 2 limes

2 shallots, peeled

1 tablespoon runny honey

Briefly whiz all the ingredients in a food processor—not too finely, so that you can still make out the ingredients. Spoon into a bowl and serve.

Index